FOLLOWING THE WAY

A Field Manual for God Seekers

Richard Ray Beavo

WESTBOW
P R E S S®
A DIVISION OF THOMAS NELSON
& ZONDERVAN

WestBow Press books may be ordered through booksellers or by contacting:

WestBow Press
A Division of Thomas Nelson & Zondervan
1663 Liberty Drive
Bloomington, IN 47403
www.westbowpress.com
1 (866) 928-1240

Scripture taken from the NEW AMERICAN STANDARD BIBLE®, Copyright
© 1960,1962,1963,1968,1971,1972,1973,1975,1977,1995 by The
Lockman Foundation. Used by permission. www.Lockman.org"

Scripture taken from the King James Version of the Bible.

ISBN: 978-1-9736-6325-6 (sc)
ISBN: 978-1-9736-6327-0 (hc)
ISBN: 978-1-9736-6326-3 (e)

Library of Congress Control Number: 2019907106

Print information available on the last page.

WestBow Press rev. date: 7/29/2019

Review by Michael Hammond

November 15, 2018

As a friend and brother in Christ for more than four decades it has been a pleasure and joy to observe your walk with the Lord. We have had immeasurable conversations and discussions about our daily life, but more importantly we have discussed the **Scripture** with great energy and at times with great debate. However, we have never wavered in our awe, respect and conviction of the inerrant, infallible **Scriptures, God's Word**. When you started writing this book, I wasn't sure what it would be about, but when you began to tell me about its contents I was not surprised. We have discussed most of its contents over these many years.

I know personally you spent years studying and researching the Scriptures concerning: The Followers of The Way. You have chewed on this concept for a long time. This topic has been a part of our conversations for decades and I am so glad you followed your heart and the leading of the Holy Spirit into putting your thoughts down on paper. You are to be commended for your diligence and effort to stay biblically sound in your research and the writing of this book.

Before I read this book I had not really paid much attention to references of "The Followers of The Way." I believe all who read this book will gain a much greater knowledge, understanding and interest in "The Followers of The Way." But most importantly one will come away with a greater desire to be a more devoted follower of "The Way", Jesus Christ.

In God's Grace,
Michael Hammond

I dedicate this book, *Following the Way*, to my grandparents:

Charles M. Way, October 12, 1881 – December 9, 1962
Eva Kilgore-Way, December 27, 1888 – May 18, 1956

They raised me from birth until I was 11 years of age. I will be eternally grateful for the start in life which they gave me and my brother Robert. They sacrificed their retirement years to raise two boys who would have otherwise had a totally different foundation for the rest of their lives.

From The Author

King David encouraged his son Solomon to get to know his father's God. He told his son to willingly serve God with all of his heart because God sees his true desires and understands his thoughts. Drawing from his own life experiences, David passed on to his son the assurance that if he sought God, He would let him find Him.

I first heard about God through Sunday School at the little brick Presbyterian Church in the village where I was raised by my grandparents. Years later, I sought the God of whom David spoke and found his admonition to be true. That was almost 60 years ago and now I am passing on to you that same assurance that if you will seek my Heavenly Father with all of your heart (because He sees your true desires and understands your thoughts) then God will also let you find Him. Finding a *true* knowledge of Him will be the greatest thing that could possibly happen to you in this lifetime.

Whenever I have desired a closer personal relationship with Him, He has faithfully revealed more of Himself to me. One morning He gave me a passage in the Bible which told me that as long as I was actively making certain things a part of my lfe, our relationship would continue to deepen. WOW!!! I had read that book before, but had never recognized that promise!!! So I had to know what those things were. Incorporating them transformed my life from a state of serving my Lord by being a good Church member to one of enjoying a growing personal Father / son relationship with God. I also began learning what my Lord Jesus is really like and experiencing the fruits of God's Spirit in my life as I placed more control in His hands and relied more on His powers.

As you read this book, my exhortation to you, the reader, is to concentrate your attention on the God that you'll be reading about, and on your own personal relationship with Him through Jesus the Messiah. I will be sharing the things that promoted and helped my own relationship to grow, and the things that demoted and hindered the intimacy of that relationship. As you read, I exhort you to do as the Bereans, who checked out the things Paul was declaring about the Christ against the Scriptures, eager to see if they could be so. With that effort and attitude, you will find the same God many of the Bereans found; and the same hope, inner strength, and power of God that many of the Bereans discovered. The account of Scripture calls the Bereans more noble minded because they were eager to know more about God and checked everything they were told against the Scriptures. I have included many Scripture quotes in the book because it is my desire that you don't just read what I have to say, but that you become familiar with what God has to say to you. Seek Him and He will let you find Him.

As I write this book I can relate to the Apostle Peter as he stated the reason for writing the first chapter of his second letter to Jesus' followers. Likewise, God has given me those same three objectives:

First, to be always ready to speak out for the Way;

Second, to be mindful of the dwindling time I have left on this earth to declare these truths; and

Third, to diligently record these things as they affected me so that after my time on this earth has expired this declaration will continue to ring out loud and clear to anyone who has eyes to read and a heart inclined toward discernment and understanding.

Richard Ray Beavo

Contents

Section 1: *Being a follower of the Way*

Section 2: *Special Messages from the Leader*

Preface

This book is divided into two major sections:

✓ The first five chapters are about being a follower of the Way.

- The First Followers Of The Way – follows the use of the term in the early records.
- Becoming A Follower Of The Way – is a description of how to become a follower of the Way.
- Following The Way – describes the way to be a follower of the Way.
- Characteristics Of A Follower Of The Way – reveals the seven characteristics which are necessary to obtain a true knowledge of Jesus, the Way.
- The Compass For Followers Of The Way – the individual goal of a follower of the Way

✓ The last four chapters are special messages which Jesus wants His followers to be aware of.

- A New Commandment For Followers Of The Way – the way all men will be able to distinguish who Jesus' followers are.
- The Enemies Of A Follower Of The Way – reveals the opposition to a follower of the Way.
- The Tools Of A Follower Of The Way – describes the tools available for living a victorious life as a follower of the Way.
- Prayers Of A Follower Of The Way – describes the communication between the Way and His followers.

Three Appendixes are also supplied for reference with the Greek word listed along with the pronunciation and a brief description of what that word means in the Greek language.

- Appendix A contains a description of each of the deeds of the flesh as listed by the Apostle Paul in Galatians 5:19–21.
- Appendix B contains a description of each of the fruits of the Spirit of God as listed by the Apostle Paul in Galatians 5:22–23.

- Appendix C contains a description of each of the character qualities of biblical love which the Apostle Paul listed in 1 Corinthians 13:4–7.

Following are some keys that I have incorporated into the book which hopefully will assist you in properly gleaning the message which I have attempted to present.

| Right and left borders | = Quotes from the Scriptures. Unless otherwise indicated, all quotes are from the New American Standard Bible. I have removed verse numbers for easier reading and because they were not in the text as it would have been read by the early believers. In many places I have also inserted new lines and tabs into the quote in order to make the meaning of the text more visible; especially in the case of conversations or lists.

[note] = Explanatory notes inserted into a Scriptural quote.

ALL CAPS WORDS = In the text of a New Testament scripture quote, the all caps words are those which the author is quoting from the Old Testament

Capitalized words = As in many English translations of the Scriptures, I have capitalized words which make a direct or indirect reference to the God of the Bible.

Italicized words = In the text of the book, *italics* are used according to proper style to indicate emphasis for the *italicized* words.

However, according to the style chosen by many modern translators, in quotes of the Scriptures italics are used to indicate that the word is not literally in the Greek or Hebrew text, but is needed to give a proper English rendering of the message.

In footnotes, italics are used to indicate the words which define the meaning of the footnoted text.

Outline forms = This book is intended as a cross between a book and an operating manual, so in many places I have departed slightly from the proper book style and used outline forms, numbered texts and emboldened headings in order that sections may be found more easily when leafing back over the pages to find out, "What did it say about _____?"

DO RIGHT
Richard Ray Beavo

It's easy to find the right thing to do,
    it was declared by a Baptist of old;
If I would only believe in Christ's name,
    it would happen just as it was told.
When I placed my trust in Him,
    He saved me from all of my sin,
He made me a part of God's family
    and cleans up my life from within.

It's easy to find the right thing to do,
    God's Spirit now dwells in my heart.
If only I'd let Him be in control,
    He'd show me where I should start.
"Love the Lord with all of my heart,
    all of my soul and all of my mind."
Then "love my neighbor as myself"
    and all the right things to do I will find.

It's easy to find the right thing to do,
    God has written it in His word.
If I would only search there I'd find
    the truth by my heart would be heard.
As I read and apply His words to my life,
    each step down His paths He will light;
I will grow like a tree well watered and fed
    and prosper with the fruit that is right.

It's easy to find the right thing to do,
    it's as clear as the nose on my face.
If I could only apply to myself
    the same deeds I'd have others embrace.
If "do unto others as I would have them
    do unto me" is the rule of my hand;
Then the Lord's mighty mysterious ways
    I'll finally begin to understand.

SECTION 1

Being a follower of the Way

Chapter 1

The First Followers Of The Way

The early believers in Jesus the Christ (or properly, the Messiah) came to be known as "followers of the Way." The Scriptures don't directly state why they were referred to in such a manner, but several things are clear from the New Testament writings.

It is completely understandable that the Apostles and the early believers would refer to themselves (and be referred to by others) as followers of the Way. They had been taught "the way" by John the Baptist and Jesus. Then they had been commissioned by Jesus, the One who declared Himself to *be* the Way, and the Truth, and the Life.[1]

That seems to have been the self-imposed distinction of the movement for quite a period of time. They did, of course, acquire other names along the way. They were referred to as "the sect of the Nazarenes" by the lawyer for the high priest, Tertullus.[2] They were also first called "Christians" at Antioch.[3] The name Christian is the name that stuck with the movement as it transformed from a Jewish sect to a worldwide movement and the name which remains to this day. While the names by which they were referred to varied, the description of their teachings, lifestyle, and living leader remained for some time as "followers of the Way." To be a member of the movement was to become a follower of the Way.

The resurrection was considered by the apostles to be a very important confirmation concerning the teachings of "the way." When Paul wrote to the Corinthian followers he told them that after being resurrected Jesus had not only appeared to His apostles but had also appeared to over five hundred people at one time. He stated that although some of those five hundred had died, the

---

[1] John 14:6
[2] Acts 24:5
[3] Acts 11:26

1

majority of them were still alive to that day.[1] Paul was basically stating to the Corinthian assembly of followers of the Way that if they wanted confirmation as to what he was telling them concerning Jesus' resurrection they could go ask some of the eyewitnesses, most of whom were still living at the time of his writing to them.

One person who seems to have taken Paul up on his challenge was Luke, most likely a Gentile follower of the Way, who stated in his writings that he felt it was necessary for him to record the results of his thorough investigation in consecutive order so that his readers would know the accurate truth about what was being taught concerning Jesus' life and ministry.[2] He wrote a Gospel book recounting the life and teachings of Jesus then went on to write the book of Acts where he recorded much of the history of the movement during those early years.

Jesus Declared Himself the Only Way to God

John 14:1–6

[Jesus speaking] "Do not let your heart be troubled; [3]believe in God, believe also in Me. In My Father's house are many dwelling places; if it were not so, I would have told you; for I go to prepare a place for you. If I go and prepare a place for you, I will come again and receive you to Myself, that where I am, *there* you may be also. And you know the way where I am going."

Thomas said to Him, "Lord, we do not know where You are going, how do we know the way?"

Jesus said to him, "I am the way, and the truth, and the life; no one comes to the Father but through Me."

---

[1] 1 Corinthians 15:6
[2] Luke 1:3–4
[3] Or *you believe in God*

Not only did Jesus declare that He is the way to God the Father, but it is important to note that He went on to declare that there is no other way to get to the Father. This discourse took place during the Last Supper where He shared much information with His disciples prior to being crucified. At the time Jesus made the above statement Judas Iscariot had just left to perform his dastardly deed. Jesus was explaining to the remaining eleven apostles what they needed to know about the coming events surrounding His impending departure from this life.

Jesus had demonstrated and taught them for the past three and a half years the way to live and minister in a God-pleasing manner, as is evident from His statement that they "know the way." Then He declared to them that He *is* that way. As Jesus their mentor had shown them on many occasions, this way was very different from the way that the Jewish religious leaders were living and conducting their ministries. The major difference is that He had demonstrated for them how to live in a close personal relationship with God, submitted fully to the leading and empowerment of the Holy Spirit. And now He had shifted gears to the final preparations for His departure and their upcoming commissioning.

They had begun the journey as believers who received Jesus as their expected Messiah. Then they progressed to being disciples, or learners, who approached Jesus' teachings with a learner's attitude. A disciple is one who is willing to expend physical and mental energy to understand and apply His teachings to their life. Then one morning, after spending a whole night in communication with God, Jesus separated twelve individuals from His disciples and named them Apostles. Those twelve would travel with Him; they would go out and preach for Him; and they would have the authority to cast out demons in His name.[1] Twice He sent disciples

---

[1] Mark 3:13–19 and Luke 6:12–16

out on mission trips[1] and then at that last supper He began final preparations for their ministry to evangelize the whole world.[2]

After supper their leader, who had made the statement that He was "the [only] way ... to the Father" was arrested and crucified. If that had been the end of the story, Jesus' statement and His teachings would most likely have suffered the same fate as other teachers who had gathered followers before Him.

> Acts 5:36–39 – a Pharisee named Gamaliel speaking,
>
> "For some time ago Theudas rose up, claiming to be somebody, and a group of about four hundred men joined up with him. [3]But he was killed, and all who [4]followed him were dispersed and came to nothing. After this man, Judas of Galilee rose up in the days of the census and drew away *some* people after him; he too perished, and all those who [5]followed him were scattered. So in the present case, I say to you, stay away from these men and let them alone, for if this plan or [6]action is of men, it will be overthrown; but if it is of God, you will not be able to overthrow them; or else you may even be found fighting against God."

But that wasn't the end of the story. Jesus demonstrated to them in an undeniable way that what He had taught them really was *the truth* and that He really was *the life* which comes from God by coming back from death and making appearances on earth for more than forty days in His resurrected body. Jesus had done what no teacher before or since Him has been able to do. That resurrection was the single most important event in history and it set in concrete for these early believers that they were not following

---

[1] Commissioned and sent out – 12 sent (Matthew 10:1–11:1; Mark 6:7–13, 30; Luke 9:1–6, 10a) and 70 sent (Luke 10:1–24)
[2] Mark 16:15
[3] Lit *Who was killed*
[4] Lit *were obeying*
[5] Lit *were obeying*
[6] Or *work*

the teachings of a leader who was dead and gone but rather a leader who was alive and had power and authority beyond anything any of them had ever previously imagined.

That is what they meant when they referred to themselves as followers of the Way. In that title they were stating that they were not just following the teachings of a good but departed leader, but that they were following a leader who was alive and well. A leader who was able to give them the true life which comes from God, lead them in the ways of their Heavenly Father, and take them into the presence of the true God.

The Way Became Widely Known

1. Saul described believers whom he was persecuting

> Acts 9:1–2
>
> Now [1]Saul, still breathing [2]threats and murder against the disciples of the Lord, went to the high priest, and asked for letters from him to the synagogues at Damascus, so that if he found any belonging to the Way, both men and women, he might bring them bound to Jerusalem.

Luke, who had made it a point to carefully investigate everything pertaining to Jesus' life and ministry,[3] indicated in this passage that Saul, a member of the Pharisee party,[4] would refer to members of the movement as "belonging to the Way." By the time of that event, "the Way" had become a definite movement within the Jewish community. Under the leadership of the twelve Apostles (minus Judas who had turned aside and plus Matthias who was selected to replace him)[5] their numbers had grown exponentially.

---

[1] Later called Paul
[2] Lit *threat*
[3] Luke 1:3
[4] Acts 23:6
[5] Acts 1:24–28

2. The believers in Jesus used the term

> Acts 18:24–26
>
> Now a Jew named Apollos, an Alexandrian by birth, [1]an eloquent man, came to Ephesus; and he was mighty in the Scriptures. This man had been instructed in the way of the Lord; and being fervent in spirit, he was speaking and teaching accurately the things concerning Jesus, being acquainted only with the baptism of John; and [2]he began to speak out boldly in the synagogue. But when Priscilla and Aquila heard him, they took him aside and explained to him the way of God more accurately.

In this passage Luke referred to the teachings of the movement in a more detailed manner. He called them instruction "in the way of the Lord," and indicated that they are "the way of God." The passage also relates the term "the way of the Lord" to the teachings of John the Baptist.

3. Enemies of the Apostle Paul used the term

> Acts 19:8–9 – Paul at Ephesus
>
> And he [Paul] entered the synagogue and continued speaking out boldly for three months, reasoning and persuading *them* about the kingdom of God. But when some were becoming hardened and disobedient, speaking evil of the Way before the [3]people, he withdrew from them and took away the disciples, reasoning daily in the school of Tyrannus.

Even the enemies of the movement (those who had "hardened" their hearts and become "disobedient" to the teachings of Paul) were described by Luke as referring to the movement with that same term, "the Way."

---

[1] Or *a learned man*
[2] Lit *this man*
[3] Lit *multitude*

4. The Apostle Paul making his defense before Felix

> Acts 24:14
>
> [Paul speaking] "But this I admit to you, that according to the Way which they call a sect I do serve [1]the God of our fathers, believing everything that is in accordance with the Law and that is written in the Prophets;"

When the Apostle Paul made his defense before Felix, the Roman appointed governor, he referred to the manner in which he served "the God of our fathers" as "the Way." Luke also revealed to us in this passage that the religious leaders who had brought an accusation about Paul considered "the Way" to be another "sect" of the Jewish religion.

It needs to be revealed here, however, that some theologians translate the Greek word for sect, HAIRESIN, into the English word "heresy." While Paul's accusers would probably have agreed that the teachings of the Way were what we now refer to as heresy, it is not consistent to translate it thus. The same Greek word is used later in Acts 26:5 to refer to the group of Pharisees which Paul belonged to prior to his conversion, and Paul most certainly would not have called that group a heresy as we think of it today. But they would definitely have called it a sect; or a distinct group, as we would today refer to a denomination or a political party.

5. Felix had prior knowledge of "the Way"

> Acts 24:22a
>
> But Felix, [2]having a more exact knowledge about the Way, put them off

Felix, a Roman official, already had "a more exact knowledge about the Way." As a Roman governor, it was his business to

---

[1] Lit *the ancestral God*
[2] Lit *knowing more accurately*

know what was going on in the community, and it appears that he was well enough informed about the followers of the Way not to accept just any definition that was brought before him.

Summary

Jesus had taught His followers that God was their Father. He is quoted as saying that His followers could approach God in the intimacy of a Father / child relationship.[1] Not just through an intermediary religious system, but on an individual basis through a living mediator.[2] Then, while this teaching was still fresh in their minds and hearts, He gave them the proof by His resurrection from the dead that His teachings were true.

For the early believers the way was much more than a set of beliefs. It was a personal relationship with God the Father through Jesus, His resurrected Son who was at the right hand of God as proclaimed by Peter,[3] seen by Stephen,[4] and later witnessed by John.[5] And the teachings were not just something that they had accepted and taught as the truth, but their accuracy and trustworthiness had been proven by the resurrection of Jesus from the dead. He had proven that He was the life which came from God Himself.

There had been others before Him who had previously claimed to be someone important, and they had gathered followers who believed their teachings. But each had died and been buried, after which their followers dwindled away.[6] But this time was different!!! This time the Leader returned from the dead in a resurrected body and spent an extended time with His followers teaching them additional things about the kingdom of God.[7] Then He told them

---

[1] Matthew 6:5–18
[2] 1 Timothy 2:5
[3] Acts 2:33
[4] Acts 7:55
[5] Revelation 4 and 5
[6] Acts 5:34-39
[7] Acts 1:3

that all of the authority in heaven and on earth had been given to Him by God and assured them that He would always be with them.[1]

When followers of the Way had followed Jesus' teachings, they had experienced the power and authority of a new life lived in Christ. Paul described that new life in his second letter to the Corinthians.[2] That new life was so dynamic that others who knew them saw the difference and wanted to have it also.

---

[1] Matthew 28:18–20
[2] 2 Corinthians 5:17

Chapter 2

Becoming A Follower Of The Way

The Scriptures are very clear about how a person becomes a follower of the Way.

The Heavens Declare the Glory of God

The early followers of the Way did not stop with just receiving Jesus by believing in His name and becoming a child of God positionally. Under the teaching of the Apostles they were directed in the process of developing a close individual relationship with their new adoptive Father in Heaven.

> 1 John 1:3–7
>
> what we have seen and heard we proclaim to you also, so that you too may have fellowship with us; and indeed our fellowship is with the Father, and with His Son Jesus Christ. These things we write, so that our joy may be made complete.
>
> This is the message we have heard from Him and announce to you, that God is Light, and in Him there is no darkness at all. If we say that we have fellowship with Him and *yet* walk in the darkness, we lie and do

not practice the truth; but if we walk in the Light as He Himself is in the Light, we have fellowship with one another, and the blood of Jesus His Son cleanses us from all sin.

1. Desire a personal relationship with God

Let us start at the beginning. The writer of Hebrews states that even though His followers can't see God, they can come to Him. They can have an active relationship with Him just as the witnesses of the Bible if they have faith that He exists and that He will reward them with His presence as they seek Him.[1]

In order to have a close personal relationship with anyone, including God, there must be a mutual desire for the relationship. God desires

> Now faith
> is the assurance
> of things hoped for,
> the conviction of
> things not seen.
> (Hebrews 11:1)
>
> ## FAITH
>
> And without faith
> it is impossible to please Him,
> for he who comes to God
> must believe that He is
> and that He is
> a rewarder
> of those who seek Him.
> (Hebrews 11:6)

Faith is the Victory

that kind of a relationship with everyone He created, but the desire must be mutual in order for it to grow and develop.

Once I was visiting a group of teens in a detention facility and asked them, "Who has received Jesus as your personal Savior?" All of the hands went immediately into the air. I was at a state juvenile detention facility, and participation in the meeting was voluntary, but I had not expected that kind of a response. The unanimous response took me back for a moment, as I was prepared to give a talk on why they should receive Him. Now they had punched a big hole in my balloon.

---

[1] Hebrews 11

The Holy Spirit came through for me and as I recovered from the shock He led me to respond with a second question, "Who would like to get to know Jesus better?" No hands. I had expected that they wouldn't all raise their hands, but I was totally unprepared for none!!!

Now this combination of responses had really sparked my curiosity, so I followed with a third question, "If you aren't interested in knowing Jesus, why did you receive Him?" There was no hesitation, as they all raised their hands shouting, "I don't want to go to hell!!!" The tone of their voices revealed their amazement that I would ask such a dumb question.

The Apostle John wrote that those people who received Jesus were given the right to be children of God and that they weren't born out of anything earthly but out of God's will for them.[1]

I have yet to find any legitimate indication that the Apostles presented the Gospel to anyone as just "Fire Insurance" or as a "Get Out Of Hell Free" card. They presented the gospel as an opportunity to experience a new life as a child of God with all the benefits that new relationship included.

2. Receive Jesus the Christ (Messiah)

Paul wrote to the Ephesians about the salvation which God offers.

> Ephesians 2:8–9
>
> For by grace you have been saved through faith; and [2]that not of yourselves, *it is* the gift of God; not as a result of works, so that no one may boast.

---

[1] John 1:12–13
[2] I.e. that salvation

Nothing anyone can do will purchase a relationship with God. God has already done everything that is needed. The Greek word translated here as "by grace" is CHARITI. It is pronounced khar-it-ee, which looks and sounds very much like the English word charity. The biblical concept of grace is also very similar to the English concept of charity. It is something that is given to someone in need as a free gift. God offers salvation for free, as charity. But like charity, in order to obtain the full benefit a person has to be willing to receive it.

The Apostle John recorded in his gospel that one day a Pharisee named Nicodemus came privately to see Jesus. He said that the signs Jesus was performing had convinced them that He was teaching God's message. Jesus immediately recognized the situation and cut right to the heart of the issue, declaring to the religious leader that he must be born of the flesh (as he obviously already was) and also born of the Spirit of God (which he obviously wasn't since he had come privately so no one would see him). Jesus went on to tell him that the way to be born of the Spirit of God was by believing in Himself as the only begotten (that is, born into this world) Son of God, which would affect the way he lived his life.[1]

There are two Greek words which are translated into the English word "believe":

- PEITHO means to be convinced in the person's mind. It would be more properly translated as "gives intellectual assent to."
- PISTEUO, however, means "to be totally persuaded" of something, and hence, to place confidence in it which in turn affects the person's actions.

PISTEUO is the word used by the Apostle John for believing in Jesus. Then just so that Nicodemus didn't miss the point, Jesus

---

[1] John 3:1–21

ended the lesson with a reference to the deeds and practices which he does in this lifetime.

If someone wishes to keep on living just as they were before, it will do nothing for their relationship with God to just say a prayer in order to avoid punishment; or to give an intellectual assent to the fact that there was a man named Jesus. Neither of those actions by themselves will endure the afflictions or persecutions which Jesus said will arise because of His word.[1] Nor will they enable a person to stand up to the worrys they will have in this world or the deceitfulness of wealth which Jesus warned about.[2] But if they receive Him into their life with an open heart that is willing to seek and follow Him in this life, then He will send His Holy Spirit into their life and they will have a new lease on life.

They will no longer have to live in the weakness of that old state but will have the new power and fruits of the Spirit available[3] to them. The new life will become a reality to them as they allow Him to lead them with His Spirit and become a follower of the Way.

3. **Become an adopted *child of God***

Paul did not stop with grace in his letter to the Ephesians, but followed salvation by grace through faith with the next statement.

> Ephesians 2:10
>
> For we are His workmanship, created in Christ Jesus for good works, which God prepared beforehand so that we would walk in them.

He had explained at the beginning of the letter what he meant by "created in Christ Jesus" when he stated that God had

---

[1] Matthew 13:21

[2] Matthew 13:22

[3] 2 Corinthians 5:17

predestined the fact that anyone who believed in Jesus would be adopted as a child of God.[1]

The emphasis of this predestination statement is not to say that God has determined who can or will be saved but rather a determination that any individual who receives the salvation offered through Jesus has been willed by God to become an adopted child to Himself.

Think of John 1:12–13, Ephesians 1:5, and 2 Corinthians 6:18 in the context of the United States of America's adoption process. Two methods of giving a child a home and family are the foster care system, and the adoption system.

In the foster care system the parents take the child into their family as a foster child, and accept the obligations and responsibilities that go along with that assignment. The relationship may be terminated at any time by either the government agency or the parents with a minimal amount of legal action. This system is normally thought of as a temporary arrangement, even though it may become rather long term. The foster care system offers the child only a small degree of personal security and assurance for their future.

However, in the adoption system the prospective parents petition the court for a legal adoption. The parents bear any burdens of payment and effort. And when the process is final, the judge makes a decree that the child is now a legal member of the adopting family. From that point on the parents have the same legal rights and responsibilities that they would have for a natural born child. The adoption system offers the child a large degree of personal security and assurance for their future. As far as *position* is concerned the child has the same legal rights and responsibilities as a natural born child. But as far as *relationships* are concerned it is equally the responsibility of the parents *and* the child as they grow to desire a close

---

[1] Ephesians 1:5

personal relationship with each other and be willing to provide the necessary time and effort for that to happen.

The adoption process is the one which the Scriptures describe as our relationship with our Heavenly Father, the God of creation.

According to the Ephesians 2:8–9 passage, the legal part of that process has been completely satisfied by God through Jesus and given to His followers as a gift by grace (God's charity), through faith. That gives the individual great personal security as they realize that being positioned as a child in God's family is not determined by what they have done or will do. It is determined by what God has done and will do.

But being part of a family also has a relational aspect to it. Relationally, both the parent and the child have responsibilities for the development of a close personal relationship. The parent and the child must each desire, and be willing to make the effort required for that relationship to grow. Like the personal relationships between any two individuals, the relationship between God the Father and His adopted child will only grow as they both do their part.

Here again, God has already demonstrated His desire for the development of the relationship and provided that individual with everything that they will need to do their part.

A. **God's demonstrations:**

1) **Old Testament examples**

God's dealings with the people in the Old Testament are summarized in Hebrews 11. According to Hebrews 12:1, they were recorded and have been preserved as demonstrations of the relationship which God desires.

2) **Jesus' life and teachings**

The life and teachings of Jesus are described in the four Gospels; Matthew, Mark, Luke, and John. According to Hebrews 12:2, Jesus is the author and perfector of a life of faith. Therefore, the demonstration of what a close relationship with God is like can be observed by studying the recorded accounts of His life.

3) **The resurrection of Jesus**

According to Romans 1:4, God has confirmed that Jesus was His son, and demonstrated that He is able and willing to carry out the rest of His promises by resurrecting Jesus from death.

B. **God's provisions:**

1) **His Spirit**

Galatians 4:6 informs the follower of the Way that the ability for constant Father / child communication between the Heavenly Father and the adopted child is provided by God through the ministry of His Spirit who dwells in the child's inner being.

2) **His Revelation**

God has provided a true revelation of Himself through Jesus. Through a *true knowledge* of Jesus, God has provided His adopted child with a *true knowledge* of their Heavenly Father. Everything that the child needs to know about their Father in order to live in close communion with Him will be provided.[1] If a follower diligently seeks a *true knowledge* in order to know Him and have a close personal relationship with Him then their Father will reveal Himself to them.[2]

---

[1] 2 Peter 1:3
[2] 1 Chronicles 28:9

3) **His Promises**

According to 2 Peter 1:4, God has provided His adopted child with many promises through Jesus in order that they can become a good child.

4) **His Word, the Scriptures**

According to 2 Timothy 3:16–17, God actually inspired the writers of the Scriptures (the Bible) in order to provide His children with the knowledge that they needed in order to have a close personal relationship with Him and live a life that is pleasing to Him.

All that is left for the relationship to grow and develop is for the adopted child of God to be willing to invest the time and effort required. That is what John wrote about in the introduction to his Gospel.

> John 1:12–13
>
> But as many as received Him, to them He gave the right to become children of God, *even* to those who believe in His name, who were [1]born, not of [2]blood nor of the will of the flesh nor of the will of man, but of God.

The Greek word used by the Apostle John which is here translated as "right" is EXOUSIA. It means "authority", such as the authority one has been given to act under the power of a higher authority. Under the law, it means lawful authority, such as the authority given to a legally adopted child to participate in a family as a full fledged child. As used here, since "He" is Jesus, it means that Jesus has given "as many as received Him", and even "those who believe in His name", all of the authority they need "to become children of God."

---

[1] Or *begotten*
[2] Lit *bloods*

My parents were divorced before I can remember, so my brother and I were raised by my grandparents on my mother's side of the family. We attended a little brick Presbyterian Church in our small village. In the Sunday School classes I was taught that there was a God who had created everything that exists. I was also taught many of the stories that are in the Scriptures. When I was eleven and one half years old, my grandmother fell, was taken to the hospital, and soon died.

Because my brother and I were foster children in our grandparents' home, the authorities removed us and placed us with my birth father's new family in the neighboring town. We had never even heard of him before that time, and the environment was the exact opposite of the quiet, safe home we had been raised in with our grandparents. I was a strong willed child, and did everything I could to express my dissatisfaction with this arrangement.

After two and one half years I ran away from home and in a few days found myself in a locked room with bars on the windows at a Juvenile Detention Facility. I had expressed my intent never to go back to my father's family, but at the same time had no idea what was in store for me from that point on. Thinking about my past, and my uncertain future, in a moment of desperation, I cried out with many tears and deep sobbings to the God whom I had heard about, "If you are, why did my Gramma have to die? And why can't I know for certain that you exist?"

A few days later, having received no immediate answer and having decided in my mind that there must not be a God, I was killing time when a call came over the PA system for me to report to the visitor center. There, I was surprised to find one of my eighth grade teachers. I later learned that the Holy Spirit had impressed upon his heart to find out what had happened to that unruly boy who sat in the back of his English class.

After introductions, he told me that he had come to inform me that there was a God, and that this God loved me very much. I had, since my grandmother's death, developed a fairly bold mouth. While preparing to inform the teacher that he was delusional because there was no God, that same Holy Spirit unmistakably impressed upon my heart that this was God's response to my questions a few days earlier. The teacher went on to tell me that my sins came between me and God, but that Jesus had paid the penalty for those sins so that I could become a child of God. When he told me that all I needed to do was receive Jesus as my personal savior, I said yes and with the teacher's direction told God that was my desire. Immediately the insecurity and turmoil that was inside me were replaced as the Holy Spirit entered my life with His peace, the assurance that there was a God, and that He is a personal being Who cares enough about me to answer when I call to Him.

The teacher and the foster homes he arranged for me to be placed into in the coming years were all members of a Bible Church, which became my home church. I learned many things about my Father God during those years, but the personal relationship did not really begin to grow from my perspective until years later when a young pastor asked me if I would like to be part of a discipleship program he was conducting. I said yes, and he guided and encouraged me in developing a habit of regular reading, study, and memorization of the Scriptures. He also encouraged regular quiet times with God, a prayer life, and the application of the new things I was learning in the Scriptures to my life. During those months, I began to know my Father in Heaven and His Son Jesus on a much more personal level as He revealed Himself to me through His Word, the Bible.

Things between me and my Father in Heaven have had their ups and downs during the years since that time, but He has always fulfilled His part for the development of a growing personal relationship. The variation has always been on my part, as I insisted on learning some things the hard way.

The development of a close personal relationship takes both time and effort. The next chapter describes the *way* that Jesus taught the Apostles, the Apostles taught the early followers of the Way, and the Apostle Peter wrote down so that it would be available to future followers.

Chapter 3

Following The Way

Jesus taught and demonstrated for those who would follow Him how to live, think, and walk in a manner that was pleasing to their Heavenly Father.

The way to live

Paul wrote to the Corinthians,

> 2 Corinthians 5:14–15
>
> For the love of Christ controls us, having concluded this, that one died for all, therefore all died; and He died for all, so that they who live might no longer live for themselves, but for Him who died and rose again on their behalf.

This is a very important concept for the follower of the Way to understand. "He died for [believers], so that they who [now] live might no longer live for themselves, but for Him who died and rose again on their behalf." There are three very important issues addressed in this short passage:

Jesus loved believers and died on the cross:

First – to pay the penalty for their sins

Past sins, present sins, and future sins, the penalty has been paid. There is no longer a penalty due. Paul wrote to the Romans that a person who has placed their faith in Jesus has peace with God through Him and that it is through faith in Him that they have obtained the grace of God.[1] They are saved by grace (God's charity) through faith, not by any works which they could do.[2]

---

[1] Romans 5:1–2
[2] Ephesians 2:8–9

Second – so that believers wouldn't live for themselves

The reason why He died was "so that they who live might no longer live for themselves." He died so that anyone who believes in Him doesn't have to live, or provide life, for their self. That was the sin which Adam and Eve committed in the Garden of Eden. God had abundantly provided everything that they needed. But Satan convinced them that God had not adequately provided for them.[1] He basically told them that God had lied, keeping them from being like God and knowing both good and evil. But, he assured them, they could provide that better life by determining for themselves what was good and what was evil. So Eve looked and saw that the fruit on the tree was delightful and that it looked good to eat. She believed Satan that it would make her wise and she would no longer have to rely upon God to give her wisdom.[2]

They decided to provide that life for themselves, living in their own provision rather than the provision which comes from God. Paul wrote to the followers of the Way in Rome that even though they knew God, they did not honor Him by believing and obeying Him, but they acted on their futile speculations that the fruit was good to eat, delightful to look at, and able to make them wise. As a result, they lost the light of living in God's provision and began living in the same foolish darkness which their tempter Satan lived in.[3]

In the world there's a saying, "An individual better look out for their self, because nobody else will!" Well, that's not how it is in the kingdom of God. Jesus looks out for each of His believers, so that they no longer have to. He has given His life for the punishment that they deserved by living for themselves. Now each believer has the same choice that Adam and Eve had. Will they live for themselves or will they live for their Father

---

[1] Genesis 3:4–5
[2] Genesis 3:6
[3] Romans 1:21–22

in heaven. The way which Jesus taught and the way which He demonstrated in His life is to be thankful for God's provision and live for Him.

Finally – so believers could live for Him

"He died for [believers], so that they who [now] live might ... live ... for Him who died and rose again on their behalf." A believer in Jesus no longer has to worry about their own salvation. He has given it to each one as a free gift, for accepting it by a sincere faith. Now each believer is free to live for Him. Not only that, but because of the resurrection, they now have that same life living in them, which raised Him from the death of the crucifixion. Paul also wrote to the Romans that the Holy Spirit living in each person who has faith in Jesus was not just a guarantee of eternal salvation when they die, but that He was also there to give them the ability to live for God in this life.[1]

The Apostle John wrote in the beginning of His gospel that the life which comes from God was in Jesus. That life which He provided is the ability for anyone who receives Him to see the truth. Without Jesus a person is not able to comprehend the true way.[2] The life which resided in Jesus was the Holy Spirit, and now that same Holy Spirit which resided in Jesus and raised Him from the dead resides in each believer to enlighten them and empower them to live for Him.

How does a believer live for Jesus? After eleven chapters of theology for the Roman followers, Paul wrote the following:

Romans 12:1–2

Therefore I urge you, brethren,
by the mercies of God,
to present your bodies a living and holy sacrifice,

---

[1] Romans 8:11
[2] John 1:4–5

25

> [1]acceptable to God,
> *which is* your [2]spiritual service of worship.
>
> And do not be conformed to this [3]world,
> but be transformed by the renewing of your mind,
> so that you may [4]prove what the will of God is,
> that which is good and [5]acceptable and perfect.

If a person continues to live for their self, they will have to do *what they think* is good in order to earn their salvation, or in order to obtain God's favor or attention. That is a definition of legalism.

But if they do what God says is good because they love God, appreciate what He has done for them, and have faith that it is the right way to live, then they will be *proving* "what the will of God is, that which is good and acceptable and perfect" in His eyes. The difference between legalism and godly living is more about the *why* than it is about the *doing*. Why does the individual do what they are doing?

Jesus died for His followers; Jesus was raised by the power of the Holy Spirit; and Jesus has given each believer in Himself that same Holy Spirit to live in them so that they have the insight and power to live for Him. That is how a person fulfills the Great Commandment to love God with their entire heart, and with their entire soul, and with their entire mind.[6] By not living for their self, but making use of that insight and power which the Holy Spirit provides in order to live for Him and be a follower of the Way, walking the path that He has laid our for them.

For many of the first years of my life as a Christian I did not grasp that principle. I was living according to my own understanding of

---

[1] Or *well-pleasing*
[2] Or *rational*
[3] Or *age*
[4] Or *approve*
[5] Or *well-pleasing*
[6] Matthew 22:37

the principles of God's word so that God would bless my life and I would reap the benefits of God's favor.

Then one day my idea of a perfect family fell apart. It seemed that after all I had sacrificed in order to do what I thought God required of me, he had not done His part. I had given up two very desirable career opportunities in my youth because they weren't family oriented and very few who followed them were able to maintain close family relationships.

I wanted to someday have the kind of close family I had been a part of when I lived with my grandparents. I read in the Scriptures that if I trained my children in the way they should live that they wouldn't depart from it.[1] I thought I had done my best to do just that, but here I found myself with two children who resented the fact that I had sacrificed for them to attend a Christian School and a conservative Church. My relationship with my wife was also in shambles. In my eyes I had served God the best I could and He had deserted me.

So, like the prodigal son which Jesus described in Luke 15:11–13, I determined that I was done with the restrictions of the life I was trying to live. I stopped attending church, and ended up splitting up the family God had given me. I took what I could lay my hands on and struck out on my own. I squandered a lot of money seeking happiness and lived a very loose, self-gratifying life and did many things that I am not proud of (and some that I am very much ashamed of) during those days.

That lifestyle lasted for a significant period of time before I woke up one day and realized that none of what I was doing was satisfying my inner longings. I remembered the inner peace I had experienced so many years before when I had first accepted Christ as my Saviour. I wished that I could again feel the presence of God that had begun at that time. A Christian friend from my past came back into my life about that time and we ended up going with his brother to a

---

[1] Proverbs 22:6

Christian seminar in a distant city. It was there that I knealt before God and told Him in all sincerity that I had sinned against Him like the prodigal son which Jesus told about in Luke 15:21. He forgave me, and a greater peace and joy than I had known while serving Him just for God's favor filled my inner being.

Since then, with the leading and power of His Spirit, I have been able to restore most of the relationships which had been broken. But I cannot undo some of the things which I did during that time because just like with Adam and Eve, there are permanent consequences of my sins that will remain until the end of this life. God is giving me the daily strength to change what I can and to live with what I can't through the ministry of His Holy Spirit in my life.

I determined in my heart that I never wanted to go back where I had just been, and when I expressed that desire to God, he directed me to 2 Peter 1:10–11 which says that as long as I practice these things I will never stumble. I would never stumble! What a promise, I thought! Of course, after reading that, I had to know what these things are. In all of my years within Christian circles I had never heard about anything such as this. And that was the seed which God planted in my heart so many years ago to write this book.

The way to think

How a believer thinks is important. Proverbs 23:7 states that what a person is really like is determined by the way that they think. Anyone can put on a false face, but what they really are is revealed by what they allow themselves to think. Paul gave the Philippian followers of the Way a list of the kind of thoughts to allow.

Philippians 4:8

Finally, brethren,
    whatever is true,
    whatever is honorable,
    whatever is right,
    whatever is pure,

> whatever is [1]lovely,
> whatever is of good repute,
> if there is any excellence
> and if anything worthy of praise,
> [2]dwell on these things.

Paul also told the Corinthian followers that he controls his thoughts by taking each and every thought captive.[3] To take every thought captive takes a good deal of training for most people, but it goes a long way toward becoming a more effective follower of the Way. It requires learning how to simply submit each thought to Paul's litmus test. Then if the thought doesn't pass the test it must be replaced with a thought that will.

> Philippians 2:1–13
>
> Therefore
>> if there is any encouragement in Christ,
>> if there is any consolation of love,
>> if there is any fellowship of the Spirit,
>> if any [4]affection and compassion,
> make my joy complete
>> [5]by being of the same mind,
>> maintaining the same love,
>> united in spirit,
>> intent on one purpose.
> Do nothing [6]from [7]selfishness or empty conceit, but with humility of mind regard one another as more important than yourselves;
>
> do not *merely* look out for your own personal interests, but also for the interests of others.

---

[1] Or *lovable and gracious*
[2] Lit *ponder these things*
[3] 2 Corinthians 10:5
[4] Lit *inward parts*
[5] Lit *that you be*
[6] Lit *according to*
[7] Or *contentiousness*

> Have this attitude [1]in yourselves which was also in Christ Jesus, who, although He existed in the form of God, did not regard equality with God a thing to be [2]grasped, but [3]emptied Himself, taking the form of a bond-servant, *and* being made in the likeness of men.
>
> Being found in appearance as a man, He humbled Himself by becoming obedient to the point of death, even death [4]on a cross.
>
> For this reason also, God highly exalted Him, and bestowed on Him the name which is above every name, so that at the name of Jesus EVERY KNEE WILL BOW, of those who are in heaven and on earth and under the earth, and that every tongue will confess that Jesus Christ is Lord, to the glory of God the Father.
>
> So then, my beloved, just as you have always obeyed, not as in my presence only, but now much more in my absence, work out your salvation with fear and trembling; for it is God who is at work in you, both to will and to work for *His* good pleasure.

In the above passage, Paul is telling the Philippians how to think in a way that "work[s] out [their] salvation" and allows God to work in their lives. The Greek word which is translated "mind" in the first sentence is the same as the word translated "attitude" in the third sentence. In both places, the word has to do with what thoughts the person allows into their mind, so what Paul is actually telling the believer is to:

- allow thoughts of Christian unity, unity with Christ and with His other followers;
- not allow thoughts of selfishness or conceit;

---

[1] Or *among*
[2] I.e. utilized or asserted
[3] I.e. laid aside His privileges
[4] Lit *of*

- allow thoughts of humility, regarding others as more important than their self and think of how to look out for both of their interests;
- think of their self as a bond-servant to God, and be obedient to Him no matter what it costs;
- do these things when they are in private as well as in public because God is with them everywhere.

A large part of following the Way is learning to think as Jesus did and controling the thoughts that the follower allows into their mind and that they allow their mind to dwell on.

The way to walk

There is a saying which goes something like this, "If you give a man a fish, you provide him with a meal; but if you teach a man to fish you have provided him with a lifetime of meals." The following passage which Jesus taught the Apostles, and Peter wrote down so those who wished to become followers of the Way would always have it, follows that admonition.

In their writings, Peter and the other Apostles describe all kinds of things which a follower of the Way should do. But in this passage Peter reveals how to obtain a *true* knowledge of Jesus. Here he reveals how to obtain a lifetime of knowing what to do and when to do it. The closer the path which Peter describes is followed, the more *accurate* that *true* knowledge of Jesus Christ will become to His follower.

> 2 Peter 1:1–11
>
> [1]Simon Peter, a bond-servant and apostle of Jesus Christ, to those who have received a faith of the same [2]kind as ours, [3]by the righteousness of our God and Savior, Jesus Christ:

---

[1] Two early mss read *Simeon*

[2] Or *value*

[3] Or *in*

31

Grace and peace be multiplied to you in the knowledge of God and of Jesus our Lord; seeing that His divine power has granted to us everything pertaining to life and godliness, through the true knowledge of Him who called us [1]by His own glory and [2][moral] excellence. [3]For by these He has granted to us His precious and magnificent promises, so that by them you may become partakers of the divine nature, having escaped the corruption that is in the world by lust.

Now for this very reason also, applying all diligence,
    in your faith supply [4]moral excellence,
    and in *your* moral excellence, knowledge,
    and in *your* knowledge, self-control,
    and in *your* self-control, perseverance,
    and in *your* perseverance, godliness,
    and in *your* godliness, brotherly kindness,
    and in *your* brotherly kindness, love.
For if these *qualities* are yours and are increasing, they render you neither useless nor unfruitful in the true knowledge of our Lord Jesus Christ.

For he who lacks these *qualities* is blind *or* short-sighted, having forgotten *his* purification from his former sins.

Therefore, brethren, be all the more diligent to make certain about His calling and choosing you; for as long as you practice these things, you will never stumble; for in this way the entrance into the eternal kingdom of our Lord and Savior Jesus Christ will be abundantly supplied to you.

Notice the five main things which Peter wrote:

---

[1] Or *to*
[2] Or *virtue*
[3] Lit *Through which* (things)
[4] Or *virtue*

1. **A believer *has* everything they need**

   Peter says that "His divine power has granted to [believers] everything pertaining to life and godliness." God has granted to every believer in Jesus everything they need in order to live the life He wants them to live, and to be a godly person. This is not godliness in the sense that Satan described it to Eve, where she would be like God, having her own natural ability to determine what is good and evil.

   King Solomon, the son of King David, king of Israel, who was given God's wisdom, states in two of his proverbs that the way that seems right to the natural mind ends up being the wrong way.[1] But rather, it is the godliness that is the reflection of a good father as seen in the life of a good child. People use expressions like "The apple didn't fall far from the tree", and "you can tell who their parents are" to describe the reflection of a parent's influence over the children who pay attention to what they say and honor their wishes.

2. **A believer *has* it through *truly* knowing Jesus and His glory and excellence**

   Peter states that this grant comes "through the true knowledge of Him who called [believers] by His own glory and excellence." There are many voices today in the Christian community professing to have a "true knowledge" of Jesus. Since "everything pertaining to life and godliness" comes to a believer through that "true knowledge", it is of the utmost importance that they make sure that the *true knowledge* they have really is "the true knowledge of Him."

---

[1] Proverbs 14:12; 16:25

3. **His promises are to enable a believer to escape corruption**

Peter echoes Paul's declaration to the Ephesians of the purpose for God's provisions through Jesus[1] when he declares, "He has granted to [believers] His precious and magnificent promises, so that by them [they] may become partakers of the divine nature, having escaped the corruption that is in the world by lust." Here again, the idea is that the believer will start reflecting their Savior Jesus the Messiah and their Heavenly Father (the God who created everything that is) as they start escaping the lust of the world.

John wrote that a believer in Jesus shouldn't love this world and the things in it (the lusts of this fleshly body, and the lust to obtain possessions, and the tendency to boast of their abilities and accomplishments in this life because if they love those things then the love of their Heavenly Father will not be in them.[2] The lusts of the world are strong and powerful, and the only way a believer can escape them is by becoming a partaker of "the divine nature" by appropriating God's "precious and magnificent promises" to them as they determine to be followers of the Way.

4. **If a believer stops with eternal salvation they are blind or short-sighted**

If a believer stops with Ephesians 2:8–9, and doesn't go on to apply these principles to their life, Peter says that they are "blind or short-sighted, having forgotten [their] purification from [their] former sins." There are multiple places where the Scriptures declare that those who fail to show their love for God by keeping His commandments don't have eyes to see or ears to hear. To try to obtain eternal salvation without salvation from "[their] former sins" while a believer is in this life is short-sighted, and forgetful of the sacrifice

---

[1] Ephesians 2:10
[2] 1 John 2:15–16

that Jesus endured in order for anyone who would believe in Him to have eternal life. That eternal life begins now, while they are in this world, not just at death.

5. **As long as a believer practices these things they will never stumble**

A believer is told to "be all the more diligent to make certain about His calling and choosing [them]; for as long as [they] practice these things, [they] will never stumble; for in this way the entrance into the eternal kingdom of [their] Lord and Savior Jesus Christ will be abundantly supplied to [them]." That is one of the "precious and magnificent promises" mentioned above. The Greek word translated here as "stumble" means to trip and fall. Some preachers call stumbling "losing salvation", others "backsliding", and still others "making a mistake" but they all agree that it is a departure from the life which God wishes for His followers.

Whatever a person calls the process, Peter wrote that if a person has placed their faith in God's grace and "these qualities are [a part of their life] and are increasing" they need not worry about stumbling, because this is the way "into the eternal kingdom of [their] Lord and Savior Jesus Christ."

Chapter 4

Characteristics Of A Follower Of The Way

In Peter's second letter to the early believers he listed the characteristics which a follower of the Way is to supply in their faith as:

1. Moral Excellence

If a believer wants to have a true knowledge of God through Jesus then the first thing they are told to supply in their faith is "moral excellence" (or "virtue" as some translate it). A simple definition of moral excellence is "a commitment to being as good a person as possible in thoughts, desires, and actions."

SUPPLY MORAL EXCELLENCE

Paul wrote to the Philippians[1] that in their thought life, they should dwell on the things which are:

- true,
- honorable,
- right,
- pure,
- lovable and gracious,
- of a good reputation,
- morally excellent, and
- praiseworthy by God.

---

[1] Philippians 4:8

37

A morally excellent thought life is a major step towards a true knowledge of the God who sees the desires of the heart and understands every thought. That is the advice King David gave his son Solomon, whom God had chosen to be the next king of Israel:

> 1 Chronicles 28:9
>
> As for you, my son Solomon, know the God of your father, and serve Him with [1]a whole heart and a willing [2]mind; for the Lord searches all hearts, and understands every intent of the thoughts. If you seek Him, He will let you find Him; but if you forsake Him, He will reject you forever.

Solomon indicated in Proverbs 23:7 that what a person is really like is determined by the condition of their heart, not how they appear to others. Moral Excellence is not just acting moral. Excellence means penetrating through the whole person. Not just moral actions, but moral actions on the outside which shine forth from a moral character on the inside.

Moral Excellence is also not perfection. God is perfect. People are not perfect. While a person may strive for perfection with their whole being, as someone who is in a race strives to be the winner of the race, there can only be one winner (barring a tie). Jesus is the only winner in the race for Moral Excellence. His calling to each of His followers is to use what He has provided in order to complete the race, and to hear Him tell them, "[3]You have done well. Because you were faithful with a few things I will put you in charge of more things. It is a joy to have you as a follower."

To be a faithful follower of the Way and have a *true knowledge* of the One who is the Way, a believer must always strive for

---

[1] Or *the same*

[2] Lit *soul*

[3] Matthew 25:21, 23

the goal of perfect Moral Excellence, because that is how they achieve the *best that they can be*.

2. Knowledge

The second step builds on the first, and answers the question, "What is good?" This is where Jesus and all other systems (including both the irreligious and the religious) separate. There are three interrelated sources that attempt to answer that question and provide people with their interpretation of good

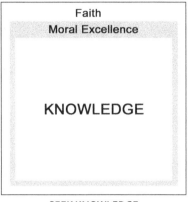

SEEK KNOWLEDGE

character. They are the world, the flesh, and the devil.

But there is a fourth source which the believer is encouraged to be personally committed to. That source is the Word of God as interpreted by the Spirit of God. The devil (often called Satan), the master of this world and inventor of the world philosophies, has no problem with people committing themselves to being good, as long as they get their definition of what is good elsewhere than from God as He reveals Himself through the Word of God by the revelation of the Spirit of God.

The Word Of God

Psalm 1

How blessed is the man who does not
    walk in the counsel of the wicked,
    Nor stand in the [1]path of sinners,
    Nor sit in the seat of scoffers!

---

[1] Or *way*

But his delight is in the law of the Lord,
And in His law he meditates day and night.
He will be like a tree *firmly* planted by
[1]streams of water,
Which yields its fruit in its season
And its [2]leaf does not wither;
And [3]in whatever he does, he prospers.

The wicked are not so,
But they are like chaff which the wind drives away.
Therefore the wicked will not stand in the judgment,
Nor sinners in the assembly of the righteous.
For the Lord [4]knows the way of the righteous,
But the way of the wicked will perish.

Years ago I memorized Psalm 1 and it has proven to be a valuable guide since. Meditation on verses or passages which I have read, studied, and/or memorized can be fit into the busiest schedule since they can be brought to mind at any time I have a down moment. There have been many times over the years that the Spirit of God has given a deeper revelation to me of how something that I have read, studied, and/or memorized applies to my life. He has also brought those verses to my mind just when I needed them to make a decision or face a trial or temptation.

The Spirit Of God

I will probably never forget the time I was driving to work and, as was my custom, was using the time to memorize Scripture verses and passages. The verse for that day was:

---

[1] Or *canals*
[2] Or *foliage*
[3] Or *all that he does prospers*
[4] Or *approves* or *has regard to*

> Romans 8:11 (KJV)
>
> But if the Spirit of him that raised up Jesus from the dead dwell in you, he that raised up Christ from the dead shall also quicken your mortal bodies by his Spirit that dwelleth in you.

I could not contain my excitement as the Holy Spirit revealed to my mind the implications of that verse. I am not normally an emotional person, but anyone who saw me that morning probably thought I was crazy as I thanked God and sang praises and worshiped Him through my tears all the rest of the way to my workplace.

God has given His Spirit to dwell inside the followers of His Son. Jesus told His disciples that after He left He would send His Father's Spirit.[1] Jesus described the Spirit of God as the Helper and the Spirit of truth. He also told them that the Holy Spirit would testify about Himself. Moments later, Jesus told His disciples that this same Spirit of truth would guide the follower of the Way into the knowledge of what is true because He would only tell about what He hears from God.[2] The Spirit of God is present in every follower of the Way and reveals God's communications to them.

In the end, and all along the way, a follower of the Way should always try to remember to rely on Him to guide them into the knowledge of what is true. They should try to always make it a priority to listen, read, study, memorize, and meditate on the Scriptures; but the strength for each of these methods comes through relying upon the Spirit of God which dwells in every believer. The follower's delight will be found in the Word of God, but the revelation of the truths contained in His Scriptures will come through the Spirit of truth. This second principle, *knowledge*, will come

---

[1] John 15:26
[2] John 16:13

41

to them through the combination of a thirst to know and the revelation of the Spirit of God.

In a follower's approach to knowledge, it is of the utmost importance to always keep in mind the goal of all their efforts, which is to mature in every way into being like Jesus.[1] It is never about just puffing one's self up by showing people how much they know and how smart they are. It is always about coming into a true knowledge of Jesus and taking their proper place within the whole body of believers.

3. Self-Control

Self-control is where "the rubber hits the road" in the life of a follower of the Way. Up till now, the follower has, in their faith, been called upon to make a commitment to moral excellence. Then to learn what God's definition of moral excellence is. But now, as a follower of the Way, self-control is calling upon the follower of the Way to apply that knowledge to their life.

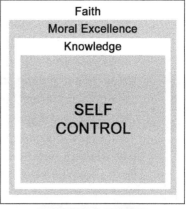

SUPPLY SELF-CONTROL

Paul wrote to the Romans and told them that they should worship God by living a sacrificial life which is acceptable to God. He told them that the way to do that was not to think as the people committed to this world think, but to think according to God's word, so that they could prove by the way they live what is good and acceptable and perfect according to God's will[2] (Romans 12:1–2).

---

[1] Ephesians 4:15b–16
[2] Romans 12:1–2

Moral excellence is what is good and acceptable and perfect according to God's will, and the follower proves it to be so by making it a part of their entire being. The goal is not just excellent actions; but excellent actions flowing from a heart that desires to be acceptable by God's standards and a mind that is filled with the knowledge of His Word.

> Galatians 5:16–18; 24–25
>
> But I say, walk by the Spirit, and you will not carry out the desire of the flesh. For the flesh [1]sets its desire against the Spirit, and the Spirit against the flesh; for these are in opposition to one another, so that you may not do the things that you [2]please. But if you are led by the Spirit, you are not under the Law.
>
> Now those who [3]belong to Christ Jesus have crucified the flesh with its passions and desires.
>
> If we live by the Spirit, let us also [4]walk by the Spirit.

Notice that the first fruit of the Spirit is love and the last fruit of the Spirit is self-control (see Appendix A & B). When God provided us with His Spirit he was providing us with the power necessary to exhibit self-control and true 1 Corinthians 13 love.

For a follower of the Way to present their body as a living and holy sacrifice is to continually resist the deeds of the flesh and exhibit the fruits of the Spirit. The passions and desires of the flesh (their life in this world) are described in 1 John 2:16 as the lusts of this fleshly body, and the lust to obtain possessions, and the tendency to boast of the abilities and accomplishments in this life. For a follower to crucify the flesh is for them to make

---

[1] Lit *lusts against*
[2] Lit *wish*
[3] Lit *are of Christ Jesus*
[4] Or *follow the Spirit*

a conscious choice not to submit to its passions and desires; but instead to live by the power of the Spirit by allowing Him to fill them instead with His fruit in their inner being (their character) and allowing that new character to control their actions.

That is the good fruit that Jesus talked about in Matthew 7:16–17. The good fruit is the fruits of the Spirit produced by walking by the power of the Spirit, and the bad fruit is the lusts of the flesh produced by not crucifying the flesh with its passions and desires.

The desire of a believer's heart is supposed to be living a morally excellent life. They should be continually filling their mind with the Word of God (the things which are good and acceptable and perfect in God's sight) and relying on the Holy Spirit for the wisdom and strength to live accordingly. Then they can say along with the Apostle Paul that they are being crucified with Christ and that it is no longer them who is living, but Christ who is living in them; and the life which they are then living in the flesh they are living through their faith in the Son of God.[1]

4. Perseverance

Now the disciple desires to be a morally excellent individual, going to God's word for knowledge, and applying the principles they find there to their life. Not just doing them, but dwelling on them with their mind and desiring them from their heart. Not from compulsion, as though they were working for their salvation or for

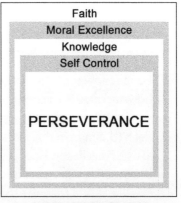

SUPPLY PERSEVERANCE

God's favor, but just because they know it's the right thing to

---

[1] Galatians 2:20

do. "Do *right* just because it's the *right* thing to do!!!" is the motto.

That was when other people begin to notice the change. Some people welcome the new person, but Jesus told His followers that they should be prepared for opposition from those who don't. Jesus warned those who would follow Him that they would meet opposition, but He said that those who lasted to the end would be saved.[1] Jesus is not talking there about just eternal salvation, but rather about saving them from the grips of a sinful nature. The context of the statement indicates that Jesus began the teaching by warning them to beware of those who would come in His name and mislead people.[2] And today there are many voices crying, "I have the real truth about Jesus!!!" and misleading many believers.

"The most dangerous lie is a half-truth!!!" For example, many deceivers quote the freedom of Ephesians 2:8–9, but completely ignore or pervert the very next verse, Ephesians 2:10, which declares that the reason a person has been saved is so that they would engross themselves in the good works of a Spirit filled life.

Some of those changes to good works will come easy over the years, but many will be very difficult and require much perseverance. Paul describes the battle thus:

> Romans 7:21–25
>
> I find then the [3]principle that evil is present in me, the one who wants to do good.
>
> For I joyfully concur with the law of God [4]in the inner man, but I see a different law in [5]the members

---

[1] Mark 13:13
[2] Mark 13:5–6
[3] Lit *law*
[4] Or *concerning*
[5] Lit *my members*

> of my body, waging war against the law of my mind and making me a prisoner [1]of the law of sin which is in my members.
>
> Wretched man that I am! Who will set me free from [2]the body of this death?
>
> Thanks be to God through Jesus Christ our Lord! So then, on the one hand I myself with my mind am serving the law of God, but on the other, with my flesh the law of sin.

But Paul didn't just leave the believer there, without any hope. He gave them the path to victory through God's Spirit working in them. That same Spirit that performed the resurrection of Jesus after His death is the Spirit that dwells in each believer in Jesus and will empower them to be victorious over sin in order to obey their Heavenly Father and live a life pleasing to Him.[3]

Victory will be found through the power of His Spirit, not through a believer's own willpower. And yet the desire and commitment of the believer is a very important factor in receiving the power of His Spirit. When the believer desires the victory *and* calls on Him, *and* allows Him to work in their life, they will see victories that they could never achieve on their own, and they can then concur with Paul, "Thanks be to God through Jesus Christ [their] Lord!"

Each follower of the Way must keep on keeping on until finally in the end we all stand before our Father in heaven, who will reward each of us according to how we did:

- to those of us who persevere in good works, eternal life;
- but to those who turn back when the going gets tough, wrath and indignation.[4]

---

[1] Lit *in*
[2] Or *this body of death*
[3] Romans 8:11
[4] Romans 2:5b–8

5. Godliness

Thus far the focus has been on what the believer in Jesus does and on the development of excellent moral character. But now the focus shifts a bit to the heart-attitude in which they do it. To supply godliness, the follower must "do *right*, with the *right* heart attitude!!!"

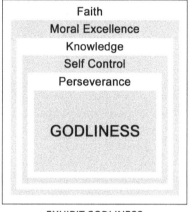

EXHIBIT GODLINESS

The Greek word used here for "godliness" is "EUSEBEIA", which means "to express one's self in reverence (deep respect from the heart) toward God and what He says." It all boils down to making it the desire of the believer's heart to walk in the Spirit; seeking to hear His voice, allowing Him to direct their life, and allowing Him to guide them in *all* their ways (thoughts, desires, and actions).

King David is a good example in the Old Testament as the Scriptures record the many times that he sought God's guidance when he had a decision to make. Many of the Psalms are attributed to his journey through life. The importance of perseverance and godliness is recorded in this description of the lives of Solomon and his father David:

> 1 Kings 11:4
>
> For when Solomon was old, his wives turned his heart away after other gods; and his heart was not [1]wholly devoted to the Lord his God, as the heart of David his father *had been*.

---

[1] Lit *complete with*

This Scripture describes David's heart as "wholly devoted to [Yahweh] his God." Here, the Scriptures record that until Solomon was old and allowed his heart to be turned away from God, he reflected the wholeheartedness with which his father David had lived for God.

Jesus is the best example to follow, as He lived His life not just in physical obedience to Our Father, but in perfect obedience which flowed from a heart of reverence and respect and thankfulness. The Greek word translated in 2 Peter 1:5 as moral excellence is the same one used earlier in the passage to describe Jesus' good character by which He provided for our salvation.[1] When the New Testament Scriptures refer to God's excellence, they use that same Greek word.[2]

The character, whether good or bad, of a parent is many times reflected in the character of their children. And that is what Peter is conveying here. The moral excellence of God the Father was reflected in Jesus as he provided for our salvation. Then Jesus' followers are called upon to, by the power and influence of the Holy Spirit, reflect that same moral excellence of their Heavenly Father's character in their character.

Godliness is not trying to be a god in the sense that Satan told Eve that she could be;[3] but it is a follower of Jesus reflecting the morally excellent character of God their Father in their life here on earth!!! There is truly a world of difference between the two. It is as great as the difference between the kingdom of this world and the kingdom of heaven.

---

[1] 2 Peter 1:3
[2] 1 Peter 2:9
[3] Genesis 3:5

6. Brotherly Kindness

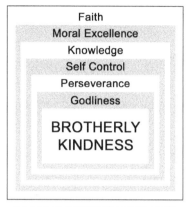

PRACTICE BROTHERLY KINDNESS

> Romans 12:10
>
> *Be* devoted to one another in brotherly love; [1]give preference to one another in honor

Brotherly kindness is the kindness and affection that a good brother or sister has toward their sibling. The Greek word for this type of love is PHILEO. That is the affectionate form of attraction. It might extend out of a person's family to the friendship they have with a close friend as they might state, "I love you like a brother (or sister)." That is the type of attraction that we are supposed to have toward our Lord Jesus the Christ [Messiah], since He is the firstborn of all of our Heavenly Father's children.[2] In that sense, everyone who has received Jesus and become a child of God[3] are brothers and sisters in the household of God the Father.

That affectionate form of love is never used in the Scriptures as a command for the believer to love God their Father. The differences between PHILEO affection and AGAPAO love, and the confusion that many of our English translators cause by using the English word love when translating both of the two Greek words, can be seen in the conversation Jesus had with Peter which is recorded in John 21:15–17.

Jesus asked Peter, in His first two questions, if he has a love towards Him that is patient, kind, unselfish, etc. as described in 1 Corinthians 13:4–7. (see Appendix C) However, in His third question and all three of Peter's responses, the translation would be more accurate as "have brotherly affection for."

---

[1] Or *outdo one another in showing honor*
[2] Romans 8:29
[3] John 1:12

We obtain our siblings through our parents. So I have one brother, a step-brother, and a step-sister in my birth father's family. Then I have many spiritual brothers and sisters through my Heavenly Father's family. Finally, I have many many brothers and sisters through my father Adam's family. Basically, this admonishment is to extend brotherly kindness to everyone around me because in one sense or another we are all brothers and sisters.

7. Love

> Matthew 22:36–40 – A Jewish lawyer speaking with Jesus
>
> "Teacher, which is the great commandment in the Law?"
>
> And He [Jesus] said to him,
> "'You SHALL LOVE THE LORD YOUR GOD
> WITH ALL YOUR HEART
> AND WITH ALL YOUR SOUL,
> AND WITH ALL YOUR MIND.'
> This is the great and [1]foremost commandment.
>
> The second is like it,
> 'You SHALL LOVE YOUR NEIGHBOR AS YOURSELF.'
>
> On these two commandments depend the whole Law and the Prophets."

It is not wise to quote Scripture verses without providing the Scripture's definition of the important terms it uses. Otherwise everyone is left to adjust the Scriptural quote to fit their own desires. I have found over the years that

Faith
Moral Excellence
Knowledge
Self Control
Perseverance
Godliness
Brotherly Kindness
LOVE

PRACTICE LOVE

---

[1] Or *first*

most people are vaguely referring to a feeling of "affection" and/or "liking" when they refer to the word love. The Scriptures are not vague in that regard.

The Apostle Paul defined AGAPAO love for us when he wrote that love :

- exhibits the inner power of patience;
- is kind in a helpful sense, gentle;
- doesn't have an inner bubbling of resentment or envy (like boiling water);
- isn't boastful, excessively self-praising;
- isn't puffed up, or having a blown up ego;
- doesn't act unbecomingly of one who claims to be a follower of Jesus, the Son of God;
- doesn't seek, desire, or demand just what is good for itself but also what is good for others;
- isn't easily aroused or incited to anger or irritation;
- doesn't keep an account, or reckon, or consider, the wrong, bad, or evil things done by others;
- doesn't rejoice, or be glad, at injustice or unrighteousness;
- rejoices, or is glad, with a true principle or belief, especially one of fundamental importance;
- covers up, hides and excuses all of the errors and faults of others;
- in an ethical sense, has all confidence in the goodness of others;
- waits for all things, including salvation, with all confidence; and
- remains against, bravely and calmly bears up against, or perseveres against all obstacles.

1 Corinthians 13:4–7 (see Appendix C)

In today's society, and particularly when dealing with Scriptures, it is important to define love, and not just leave it as a vague feeling that anyone can say "I have love!", or "You

Richard Ray Beavo

aren't loving!" when indeed they are not referring to any of the above biblical characteristics.

The problem comes into clearer focus when I realize that the language of the New Testament has three different words for love; sexual [EROS] attraction, brotherly [PHILEO] affections, and virtuous [AGAPAO] love. The first is not found in the New Testament, and both of the latter being many times translated using the English word love.

The word which is used by Jesus when answering the lawyer and the word used for the fruit of the Spirit of God is AGAPAO love, and that is the love which is defined in 1 Corinthians 13. The Scriptures are very clear here that a believer is loving, and living a Spirit filled life, to the extent that those qualities are part of their inward and demonstrated character. The chapter in Corinthians even begins by stating:

1. If a believer doesn't have and demonstrate these character qualities, anything they say is just a bunch of noise.[1]
2. If a believer doesn't have and demonstrate these character qualities, all of their knowledge and faith leaves them worthless.[2]
3. If a believer doesn't have and demonstrate these character qualities, all of their generosity is worthless to them.[3]

The Scriptures also declare that this AGAPAO love is supposed to permeate the being, showing itself in what is said, and in what is done.[4] Jesus said that the demonstration of this kind of character, not just to a believer's friends but also to their enemies, is what sets their life apart as a child of God, because it is the very character of their Heavenly Father.[5]

[1] 1 Corinthians 13:1
[2] 1 Corinthians 13:2
[3] 1 Corinthians 13:3
[4] 1 John 3:18
[5] Matthew 5:44–46

52

Chapter 5

The Compass For Followers Of The Way

> 1 Timothy 1:3b–7
>
> instruct certain men
>> not to teach strange doctrines,
>> nor to [1]pay attention to myths and endless genealogies,
>> which give rise to mere speculation
>> rather than *furthering* [2]the administration of
> God which is by faith.
>
> But the goal of our [3]instruction is [AGAPAO] love
>> from a pure heart
>> and a good conscience
>> and a sincere faith.
> For some men, straying from these things, have turned aside to fruitless discussion, wanting to be teachers of the Law, even though they do not understand either what they are saying or the matters about which they make confident assertions.

The goal of the instruction of the Apostles was AGAPAO love. Paul used the same Greek word when writing to Timothy that Peter used at the end of his list of things a believer is called to supply in their faith. The end goal is AGAPAO love. Love is not the whole instruction, it is the end goal, and to further emphasize that point Paul goes on to further define the love he is talking about in 1 Corinthians 13. He also lists that same form of love as the first fruit of the Spirit filled life.

---

[1] Or *occupy themselves with*

[2] Lit *God's provision*

[3] Lit *commandment*

This is not just a New Testament concept. In Psalm 24:3–5 the psalmist declares that if a person wishes the favor of God they must:

1. seek both outer and inner cleanliness (have a pure heart);
2. not claim that they are something that they are not (have a sincere faith); and
3. not be deceitful (have a good conscience).

To Timothy, Paul declares that every believer's objective should be to have AGAPAO love from a pure heart, a good conscience, and a sincere faith.

Love From A Pure Heart

The heart, as it is used in the Scriptures, represents the center for the inner being of an individual. As the physical heart is the center of the circulatory system, the heart is seen as the center of the inner self from which the affections, desires, and intentions shine forth. Whereas morality has to do with acting morally, moral excellence (or virtue) has to do with also being moral in the inner self, or having a pure heart.

Jesus said in the Sermon on the Mount that it is the pure in heart who will see God.[1] The concept of a pure heart in the Scriptures is not the concept of perfection, or never having been impure; but that of cleanliness, or having been cleansed.[2] In a physical sense, it is without admixture; separated from the contamination of pollutants. In a Spiritual sense, it is a clean heart, constantly purged by God through His word and the power of His Holy Spirit from the contaminating influences of sin and filled with the fruits of the Spirit of God.[3]

---

[1] Matthew 5:8
[2] 2 Timothy 2:20–22
[3] 1 Peter 1:22–23

Love From A Good Conscience

A good conscience is obtained and maintained by the application of a person's pure heart to their actions and words. Their pure heart witnesses to their conscience that their actions were good. If they have a pure heart and act in an impure manner then their good heart witnesses that they didn't do what was right to do and gives them a guilty conscience. The person's conscience is the judgments of their heart upon their thoughts and actions. That is why Paul listed a pure heart before a good conscience.

- If the heart is conformed to this physical world[1]

    o and polluted with the lusts of this fleshly body,
    o and the lust to obtain possessions,
    o and the tendency to boast of the abilities and accomplishments in this life[2]

    then the conscience will also be polluted.

- However, if the heart is

    o affectionately directed toward a *true* knowledge of Jesus[3]
    o and allowing God to transform it by filling the heart with the fruits of His Spirit

    then the conscience will also become pure and good.

When defending himself before the governor Felix, the Apostle Paul declared that because he has placed his hope in God and the fact that there will certainly be a resurrection of both the righteous and the unrighteous, he does everything that he can to always maintain a blameless conscience before God and before other men.[4]

---

[1] Romans 12:2
[2] 1 John 2:16
[3] 2 Peter 1:8
[4] Acts 24:15–16

Paul wrote to the Corinthians that he had confidence in the testimony of his conscience, that he had not conducted himself in the wisdom of his flesh, but in holiness and sincerity by the grace of God.[1]

Love From A Sincere (or un-hypocritical) Faith

The Greek word translated as "sincere" means unfeigned (not pretending), or without hypocrisy (pretending on the outside to have virtues, moral or religious beliefs, principles, etc. while not having them on the inside).

The word "faith" (PISTIS in Greek), as it is used here, is never something that is created by a believer. In the Ephesians 2:8–10 passage, the statement that it is not by their power refers to both of the previous statements; that it is by grace and that it is through faith. This is shown by the tense of the Greek word which is translated as the English word "that."

The concept that (PISTIS) faith is the gift of God is further demonstrated by Paul's statement to the Romans that faith is measured out to each person by God.[2] Paul also wrote to the Galatians that one of the fruits of the Spirit is faith.[3]

Summary

In practice, it is the believer's heart (the inner being with its affections, desires, and intentions) that

1. needs to be committed to being morally excellent
2. according to the knowledge of God's Holy Scriptures
3. as revealed by the Holy Spirit's revelation.

Then

4. the believer needs to rely upon the Holy Spirit for the power of self control and perseverance in applying that commitment to actions.

---

[1] 2 Corinthians 1:12
[2] Romans 12:3
[3] Galatians 5:22 KJV, the NASB incorrectly translates this as "faithfulness"

The more proficient a believer becomes in this process, the more

5. they will reflect their Heavenly Father's godly character; and the more
6. they will be able to PHILEO love their siblings (natural family, family in the Lord, and in the world); and the more
7. they will be able to demonstrate AGAPAO love towards God and others as much as they AGAPAO love their self.

Peter says that if a believer desires and longs for these qualities in their life and the qualities are increasingly becoming part of their character and actions then Jesus will reveal to them a *true* knowledge of Himself.[1]

This true knowledge of the resurrected Messiah and the power His Spirit gives are what creates a truly transformed life. That truly transformed life is what the early believers in Jesus meant by the term "following the Way." That truly transformed life is what made the early believers so dynamically different than their religious counterparts that their numbers grew exponentially and struck fear in the religious community of that day, causing those who refused to commit themselves to following the Way to respond with persecution in order to try to maintain their status quo.

For Jesus' followers, the new life began with a commitment to excellence; not just by acting morally (being a religious part of a synagogue, and listening to sermons by the priests, and singing emotional songs, and giving alms, and saying fancy prayers before men) but by committing their whole being to having a *true* knowledge of God as their Father in Heaven and becoming new creatures[2] reconciled to the One whose words judge the thoughts and intents of the heart.[3] Jesus taught them that "the way" is a commitment to a pure heart and a good conscience and a sincere, un-hypocritical faith. He taught them that it all begins with

---

[1] 2 Peter 1:4–8
[2] 2 Corinthians 5:17–21
[3] Hebrews 4:12

diligently committing to moral excellence as part of their faith in God their Father and Jesus their Lord.

This can be seen in the Sermon on the Mount where Jesus says:

- the pure in heart are the ones who will be able to see God their Father[1];
- the ones who will be able to enter the kingdom of heaven are those who are righteous on the inside as well as the outer righteousness of the scribes and Pharisees[2];
- having anger towards someone is as much of a pollution to a person's morally excellent character as murder is[3];
- having lust in their heart for a woman is as much of a pollution to a person's morally excellent character as committing adultery with her[4];
- a morally excellent character requires that a person must not only love and pray for those who are friendly to them, but also those who persecute them and those who make themselves their enemies[5];
- to be morally excellent a person must be constantly maturing in both their character *and* their works, because their Heavenly Father is totally mature in His character *and* the things which He does[6];
- if a person acts morally excellent just to be noticed by other people then those people's praise will be their only reward[7];
- if a person acts morally excellent without regard to who notices, just between themselves and their Father in heaven, then He will reward them[8];

---

[1] Matthew 5:8
[2] Matthew 5:20
[3] Matthew 5:21–22
[4] Matthew 5:27–28
[5] Matthew 5:43–45
[6] Matthew 5:48
[7] Matthew 6:1
[8] Matthew 6:3–4

- for a follower of the Way, prayer is simply communication between them as a child of God and their Heavenly Father[1];
- a follower of the Way's, religious service should be a personal thing between them, their fellow followers, and their Father in heaven[2]; and
- the only way to obtain a pure heart and a good conscience and a sincere, un-hypocritical faith is to keep the affections, desires and the intent of the heart on the treasures of heaven rather than the things which are on the earth.[3]

Throughout His ministry Jesus demonstrated and taught many more things pertaining to maturing in the objective of love from a pure heart and a good conscience and a sincere, un-hypocritical faith. That is why it is so important for His followers to obtain a *true* knowledge of Him and His teachings.

In Luke 19:1–10, pay particular attention to the encounter of Jesus with Zaccheus in Jericho. Remember that Levi (also called Matthew) the son of Alphaeus was also a tax collector, and had been converted and named an Apostle by Jesus some time earlier. Zaccheus could very well have known of this conversion and that would explain why he was so intent on wanting to see Jesus as He passed by. His was a true conversion of the outer life *and* the inner life (the affections, desires and the intents of the heart). And Jesus bore witness that this conversion was real (a sincere, un-hypocritical faith) when He declared that salvation had just been experienced in that house.

The "goal of our instruction" can be seen throughout the Scriptures, which contain so many more examples. Keep the goal of the teachings of the followers of the Way in mind and re-read the Old and New Testaments. This goal which begins with a desire to truly know the God of creation and results in individuals filled with and demonstrating the love of God flowing "from a pure heart and a good conscience and a sincere faith" can be clearly seen throughout the writings of the authors as they were led by the Holy Spirit of God.

---

[1] Matthew 6:5–8
[2] Matthew 6:17–18
[3] Matthew 6:19–21

SECTION 2

Special Messages from the Leader

Chapter 6

A New Commandment For Followers Of The Way

All of the love references in this chapter are for the AGAPEO love described in 1 Corinthians 13 (Appendix C) unless otherwise indicated.

The Great Commandments

During His ministry Jesus was asked which commandment of the law was the greatest by an expert in the Mosaic Law. His response was to quote Deuteronomy 6:5 which states that a person should love Yahweh their God with all of their heart, soul, and mind. He then told the lawyer that the second greatest commandment is Leviticus 19:18 which says that a person should love their neighbor in the same way that they love their self.

Then Jesus went on to state that obedience to all of the laws and the Prophets depend upon these two commandments.[1] That word "depend" is a translation of the Greek word KREMATAI which means "to be suspended from", such as grapes hanging from the grape vine. He *was not* saying that having love takes the place of obedience to the law and the writings of the Prophets. What Jesus *was* saying is that my obedience to the law and the Prophets should all be done from a love for God and a love for my fellow human beings.

---

[1] Matthew 22:40

The New Commandment

Then during the last hours Jesus spent with His followers before being arrested, He gave the Apostles (minus Judas who had just left to betray Him) a new commandment. He repeated that new commandment three times during their conversation.

First time:

> John 13:34–35
>
> "A new commandment I give to you, that you love one another, even as I have loved you, that you also love one another.
>
> By this all men will know that you are My disciples, if you have love for one another."

Second time:

> John 15:12–14
>
> "This is My commandment, that you love one another, just as I have loved you.
>
> Greater love has no one than this, that one lay down his life for his friends.
>
> You are My friends if you do what I command you."

Third time:

> John 15:17
>
> "This I command you, that you love one another."

Explanation of the New Commandment

Jesus put such a high value on this new commandment that He repeated it three times to be sure that they caught it. Before giving His life for their salvation, Jesus spent three and a half years with His followers, demonstrating His love for them in practical ways. When Jesus told the disciples, "even as I have loved you, that you also love one another", He was referring to the times He had spent discipling them.

After shedding light on the new relationship with God which Jesus' followers have through Him, the writer of Hebrews then went on to describe what their proper response to the privilege of that relationship should be. That response is a good demonstration of the relationship which Jesus had with His followers and the relationship which He commanded them to have with each other.

> Hebrews 10:23–25
>
> Let us hold fast the confession of our hope without wavering, for He who promised is faithful; and let us consider how to stimulate one another to love and good deeds, not forsaking our own assembling [gathering] together, as is the habit of some, but encouraging *one another*; and all the more as you see the day drawing near.

The believer in Jesus is told to:

1. "hold fast the confession of [their] hope [for salvation (both during this life and eternally after death)] without wavering";
2. "consider how to stimulate one another to love and good deeds"; and
3. "encourag[e] one another."

Those are the three reasons for which believers are told to gather together.

Here in Hebrews 10:25, the word translated as "assembling together" is actually the Greek word EPISUNAGOGE which means "a gathering together." The word is only used in one other place in the New Testament writings, 2 Thessalonians 2:1, in reference to the "gathering together" that will occur as Jesus' followers meet Him in the air at the rapture. This type of "gathering together" takes place any time followers of the Way meet with one another for any or all of the three purposes listed (perseverance, stimulation or encouragement). They may be *gathering* one-on-one, they may be *gathering* in a small group, or they may be *gathering* in larger groups.

Jesus told His disciples that He would be with them when ever two or three of His followers were gathered together in His name.[1]

Jesus' Example

The Scripture records reveal that Jesus followed that three point pattern in His ministry.

1. He "[held] fast the confession of [His] hope [for salvation] without wavering."
    Jesus knew that He was the promised Messiah who had been sent from God for the salvation of the world, and at the end He was able to face God and say He had accomplished the task which God had given Him. He was able to honestly say to God His Father, at the last supper He shared with His followers, that He had:

    a. finished the work which His Father had given Him to do[2],
    b. clearly shown His followers who His Father is and what He is like[3],
    c. given all glory to His Father so His followers would know that everything He has came from God[4], and
    d. helped His followers understand that He had come from God.[5]

2. Jesus had shown His followers "how to stimulate one another to love [their Father in heaven and each other] and [how to

---

[1] Matthew 18:20
[2] John 17:4
[3] John 17:6
[4] John 17:4, 6
[5] John 17:8

perform truly] good deeds [which came forth from a good character]."

3. He had encouraged His disciples many times during the three and a half years that they followed Him. Then Jesus told His core followers, the twelve Apostles, that He desired to share that last Passover with them before He fulfilled what it represented.[1] John wrote five whole chapters describing the encouragements which Jesus gave to them during that meal.[2] Then after the resurrection Jesus gave the eleven disciples (minus Judas who had betrayed Him) the commission to go everywhere making disciples, baptizing them in His name, His Father's name, and the Holy Spirit; teaching them everything which He had taught them. He began that commission with the encouragement that He had the authority to commission them and ended it with the encouragement that He would always be with them.[3]

A good example of Jesus' stimulation and encouragement can also be seen in John's record of His encounters with His first disciples:

First Day

That first day took place in Bethany beyond the Jordan. John the Baptist's disciples would surely have heard him describe himself simply as a heralder and state that the Messiah was the one whom he was heralding. They would also have been aware that forty days earlier John had baptized Jesus. They most likely would have understood that the reference John made to Isaiah's words was because the Pharisees expected Isaiah to return to herald their expected Messiah.[4]

---

[1] Luke 22:14–16
[2] John 13, 14, 15, 16, and 17
[3] Matthew 28:18–20
[4] John 1:19–28

Second Day

The next day John the Baptist pointed out Jesus to his disciples and explained to them that Jesus is the one he was sent to identify. They would surely have understood that he was identifying Jesus not only as the expected Messiah but also as the Son of God.[1]

Third Day

The third day two of John the Baptist's disciples (Andrew, Simon Peter's brother and another) were with him when he again pointed out Jesus. They left John and became Jesus' first two disciples.

The other disciple is believed by many Bible Scholars to have been John, the writer of the book. Upon coming into contact with His first two disciples Jesus invited them to spend time with Him. In other words, they *assembled together.* It is not hard to imagine the ways that He *stimulated them* and *encouraged them* during that first time together. They surely had many questions to ask Him, and He surely would have had many things that He wished to have them understand. There is one thing clear from the passage though; whatever transpired, it had such an impact upon Andrew that He didn't waste any time finding his brother and declaring that he and John had *found the Messiah.*[2]

Fourth Day

Evidently John, Andrew, and Peter were *stimulated* and *encouraged* so much from that first day with Jesus that it is likely they told Him about others whom they knew were also eagerly awaiting the Messiah such as their friend Philip. Jesus then *stimulated* and *encouraged* them even more by finding Philip and giving him an invitation to join the group.

---

[1] John 1:29–34
[2] John 1:35–42

Philip was so excited to be included as a part of the group that he went to tell his friend Nathanael. And as a result of Nathanael's skepticism Jesus performed a miracle for the group. That miracle and the ensuing discourse with Nathanael would certainly have *stimulated* and *encouraged* anyone who had been a part of their assembled group.[1]

Fifth and Sixth Days

The Gospel writer then skipped two days. Imagine the events and discussions which filled those days. They would most likely have had many opportunities *to stimulate one another* and *encourage one another*.

Seventh Day

Then, on the seventh day of the narrative, Jesus took His disciples (Andrew, Peter, John, Phillip, and Nathanael) with Himself, His mother, and maybe even His brothers to a wedding. There they had the opportunity to witness the first public sign that He was indeed the Messiah as He performed a *good deed* for the wedding couple by turning water into the wine which was needed for the celebration.

Being present at this event and seeing Jesus manifest His glory by performing the miracle certainly *stimulated* and *encouraged* these five disciples. The passage says that they now believed (the Greek word PISTEUO) in Him to the extent that they were willing to place confidence in Him and what He said.[2]

A Mini Retreat

Once Jesus' disciples had come to the place where they had confidence in what He was telling them, John informs us that He took them on a retreat along with His mother and brothers.[3]

---

[1] John 1:43–51
[2] John 2:1–11
[3] John 2:12

Imagine how *stimulated* and *encouraged* these five disciples would have been to hear the stories which Jesus' mother and brothers most likely shared with them about His birth and life up to that time. And Imagine what they probably also learned about the birth and childhood of Jesus' relative John the Baptist as well.

This passage recorded by John describes only a small portion of the examples from Jesus' life before telling His disciples, "even as I have loved you, that you also love one another."

Application of the New Commandment

Those things cannot be done if followers of the Way do not gather together. The first followers did gather together on a regular basis according to the following two records:

> Acts 2:42–47
>
> They [the early followers of the Way] were continually devoting themselves to the apostles' teaching and to fellowship, to the breaking of bread and [1]to prayer.
>
> [2]Everyone kept feeling a sense of awe; and many wonders and [3]signs were taking place through the apostles.
>
> And all those who had believed [4]were together and had all things in common; and they *began* selling their property and possessions and were sharing them with all, as anyone might have need.
>
> Day by day
>> continuing with one mind in the temple, and breaking bread [5]from house to house, they were taking their [6]meals together

---

[1] Lit *the prayers*
[2] Lit *fear was occurring to every soul*
[3] Or *attesting miracles*
[4] One early ms does not contain *were* and *and*
[5] Or *in the various private homes*
[6] Lit *food*

> with gladness and [1]sincerity of heart,
> praising God and
> having favor with all the people.
> And the Lord was adding [2]to their number day by day
> those who were being saved.

Acts 4:32–35

And the [3]congregation [whole number, multitude] of those who believed were of one heart and soul; and not one of them [4]claimed that anything belonging to him was his own, but all things were common property to them.

And with great power the apostles were giving testimony to the resurrection of the Lord Jesus, and abundant grace was upon them all.

For there was not a needy person among them, for all who were owners of land or houses would sell them and bring the [5]proceeds of the sales and lay them at the apostles' feet, and they would be distributed to each as any had need.

According to the descriptions of these meetings, they took place *in the temple, day by day,* and *from house to house.* Those two passages in the book of Acts give a brief description of what it was like for those early followers as they met to follow the Way by:

1. "hold[ing] fast the confession of [their] hope [in the transformed life which Jesus promised in this life and ultimately in the resurrection] without wavering" as they learned the *way to live;*

---

[1] Or *simplicity*
[2] Lit *together*
[3] Or *multitude*
[4] Lit *was saying*
[5] Lit *the prices of the things being sold*

2. "consider[ing] how to stimulate one another to love and good deeds" by looking out for the interests of others the same way that they would look out for their own interests[1] as they learned *the way to think*; and
3. "encouraging one another" as they practiced *the way to walk* – in a true knowledge of Jesus.

---

[1] Philippians 2:4

Chapter 7

Enemies Of A Follower Of The Way

John 15:18–21 – Jesus told His disciples,

"If the world hates you, [1]you know that it has hated Me before *it hated* you.

If you were of the world, the world would love its own; but because you are not of the world, but I chose you out of the world, because of this the world hates you.

Remember the word that I said to you, 'A slave is not greater than his master.'

If they persecuted Me, they will also persecute you; if they kept My word, they will keep yours also.

But all these things they will do to you for My name's sake, because they do not know the One who sent Me."

When a person joins God's family, they inherit a position in His kingdom and in His family. They also inherit His enemies. After telling His disciples that the way they abide in His love is by keeping His commandments just as He abided in His Father's love by keeping His Father's commandments,[2] and giving His disciples the new commandment to love one another, Jesus warned them about the enemies which they were inheriting.

The world which Jesus is describing in the above passage is not just this physical world. The Apostle John gave a description of what Jesus was referring to as *the world* in his first letter.[3] It is:

1. the lust of the flesh,
2. the lust of the eyes, and
3. the boastful pride of life.

---

[1] Or (imperative) *know that*

[2] John 15:10

[3] 1 John 2:15–17

73

The World

If a person wants to continue living in the lust of the flesh, the lust of the eyes, and the boastful pride of life then they will not receive a whole lot of trouble from the world around them because they will be thinking and acting just like the world. But if they follow the Apostle Paul's call to live a life acceptable to God by renewing their mind in order to know and follow the will of God[1] then they can expect that most likely those who are in the world who are not seeking to follow the Way by having a *true* knowledge of Jesus Christ[2], and are not concerned about entrance into Jesus' kingdom[3] will treat them in a manner similar to the way they treated Jesus. Choosing to become a follower of the Way will put a person at odds with the world that they live in.

There is a difference between being "in" the world and being "of" the world. Everyone is born into this world. They will remain *in* this world until their death. Because their most distant relatives, Adam and Eve, chose to be *of* this world, when a person is born they inherit their family's nature as members *of* this world. They inherit what is many times referred to as the "flesh" or the "sin nature."

But that isn't the end of the story. If a person makes a decision to accept Jesus as their personal Savior then they have the opportunity to be adopted into God's family. That decision makes it possible for them to no longer be "of" this world through their father Adam, but to be *of* the kingdom of God by receiving His Son into their life and exercising their right to become a child of God.[4]

The way they exercise that right is to no longer focus their affections on the things of the world (the lust of the flesh, the lust of the eyes, and the boastful pride of life) but to focus on doing the will of God which is to become a follower of His Son, the Way. That is how a follower of the Way is called to live *in* the world but not *of* the world.

---

[1] Romans 12:1–2
[2] 2 Peter 1:8
[3] 2 Peter 1:11
[4] John 1:12–13

The Flesh

Paul described the results of a person focusing their affections on the things of the world for the Galatians (see Appendix A).[1] The passage reveals that they cannot "have the best of both worlds." If they are practicing the lusts of the world then they are not living in the kingdom of God as a follower of the Way and experiencing the fruits of the Spirit in their life.

John described the fleshly tendencies which make up the "flesh" or "sin nature."[2] Those who wish to control a believer, take advantage of them, or destroy them will use those fleshly tendencies against them. It is a profitable practice for a believer to not only be aware of the existence of those tendencies, but to use them to discern the intent of messages which they receive as part of their daily life. They can recognize many advertisements, political messages, and even many religious messages which rely upon one or more of the lusts and pride that is in the world.

The reliance upon these things to convey a message should always throw up a red flag. Some times an entire message needs to be rejected because it is entirely permeated with the things of this world; the lust of the flesh, the lust of the eyes, and the boastful pride of life. Other times the message can be accepted because only the method of conveying the message is polluted. But whenever the red flag pops up it is time to do a thorough assessment of what is true and what is false.

If a believer wants to be transformed into the life of a follower of the Way by renewing their mind[3] then they will have to only allow the true part of communications into their mind and refuse to accept or dwell on the false part. Whenever that red flag is ignored and a falsehood is allowed into the life of a believer it will produce one or more of the deeds of the flesh. And the longer a falsehood is

---

[1] Galatians 5:19–21
[2] 1 John 2:16
[3] Romans 12:2

allowed to remain in a person's mind the harder it will be to get it out once it is no longer desired.

The Devil

> Ephesians 2:1–6
>
> And you [1]were dead [2]in your trespasses and sins, in which you formerly walked according to the [3]course of this world, according to the prince of the power of the air, of the spirit that is now working in the sons of disobedience.
>
> Among them we too all formerly lived in the lusts of our flesh, [4]indulging the desires of the flesh and of the [5]mind, and were by nature children of wrath, even as the rest.
>
> But God, being rich in mercy, because of His great love with which He loved us, even when we were dead [6]in our transgressions, made us alive together [7]with Christ (by grace you have been saved), and raised us up with Him, and seated us with Him in the heavenly places in Christ Jesus

In Paul's message to the Ephesians he revealed the believer's third enemy. In the above passage he is called "the prince of the power of the air" and "the spirit that is now working in the sons of disobedience." That one who is called "the prince" and "the spirit" are references to the same one who told the Lord that he had been meandering around on the earth.[8] The book of Job identifies him to be Satan, or otherwise known as the Devil.

---

[1] Lit *being*
[2] Or *by reason of*
[3] Lit *age*
[4] Lit *doing*
[5] Lit *thoughts*
[6] Or *by reason of*
[7] Two early mss read *in Christ*
[8] Job 1:7b

Paul told the Ephesians that the enemy of the follower of the Way is not human, but that it is the spiritual forces of darkness and wickedness in heavenly places (which include this world).[1] While those forces use humans as instruments to accomplish much of their ungodliness, Paul saw it necessary for believers to realize that their struggle is not against the human instruments but against the spiritual forces that are using them. And those forces are led by Satan.

Satan displayed his power of persuasion in the Garden of Eden when he twisted the words of God to fit his desires. He has used that same trick over and over throughout history. Just as he was able to even reach into the very garden which God had planted and profess his perversion of God's words to the people who walked with God in the cool of the evening, so he reaches today into all the world even including the very groups that profess to know Jesus, the Christian Churches. He gives many perversions of who Jesus is and what His words mean. Satan is an expert at using the forces of darkness and wickedness and the lusts of this world against God's people in order to accomplish his goals.

How different it might have turned out had Adam and Eve waited until the cool of the day when they again met with the Lord God and asked Him what was really good for them. How different it is today whenever a believer actually turns to Him and allows His Spirit to show them what is good and what is bad through a proper understanding of His Word. Whenever a believer actually makes the effort to take Paul's advice to the Romans in chapter 12 and verse 2 to be transformed by renewing their mind in order to prove through the way they live what is good and acceptable and perfect before their Heavenly Father then they are on the path to victory against Satan and His forces.

Very little is actually known about the laws which God set up when He created the spiritual forces in the realms of heaven. That spiritual realm is not visible to humans and is not available for scientists to

---

[1] Ephesians 6:12

research. However, God has revealed all that humans need to know about it in His word, the Bible. What is known is that the heavens were created by God in the beginning of time.[1] Therefore, God is greater than any of the spiritual forces which occupy that realm of existence.

It is also revealed by the Scriptures that it was the tree of the knowledge of good and evil which God told Adam not to eat because if he did he would die.[2] That means that a believer doesn't need to know any more about the knowledge of good and evil than what God reveals to them in His word. When Moses was giving God's instructions to the Israelites before they entered the Promised Land he told them that they were to have nothing to do with the following things[3]:

1. making children pass through fire (child sacrifice);
2. using divination, seeking knowledge of the future or the unknown by supernatural means, or by those who are saying, 'The Lord declares,' when the Lord has not sent them[4];
3. using magic, whether white or black;
4. using tarot cards, ouija-boards, astrology as an omen, etc.;
5. exercising supernatural powers through the aid of evil spirits, such as voodoo;
6. doing enchantments, particularly with a wand or hand movement;
7. acting as a go-between to communicate with the dead or the spirit world;
8. consulting the spirit world; or
9. calling up the dead, as in a séance.

God does not want His followers to seek to know about evil, but only to act and think blamelessly before their Father in heaven by concentrating on what *He* tells them to do. King Solomon, in

---

[1] Genesis 1:1
[2] Genesis 2:17
[3] Deuteronomy 18:9–14
[4] Ezekiel 13:6

the book of wisdom, wrote that if a person seeks favor with God, they should seek what is good in His eyes, but if they seek to know evil, evil will come upon them.[1] King David, in one of his psalms, says that a person should run from what is evil and concentrate on doing good; seeking peacefulness.[2] God is good and the spiritual forces of darkness and wickedness are evil so a follower of the Way would naturally prefer to seek peace with God and man and pursue it instead.

Paul wrote to the followers of the Way in Thessalonica and told them that they should carefully put everything to the test to determine if it is good or evil, then cling to the good things and abstain from the evil things.[3]

---

[1] Proverbs 11:27
[2] Psalm 34:14
[3] 1 Thessalonians 5:21

Chapter 8

Tools Of A Follower Of The Way

According to the Apostle Peter, God has given every believer, through Jesus, everything that they need to live a life of godliness.[1] Peter was writing to those people who had already placed their faith in Jesus Christ[2], so that statement means that if a person has received Jesus as their personal Savior[3] they already have available to them everything they need in order to live the life which Jesus wishes for them to live and to reflect the godly character of their Heavenly Father.

There is a modern illustration which helps in understanding this principle. A person of considerable means went to a credit company, opened an account, and gave the credit card to a needy person. They assured the needy person that whatever they charged to the card would be paid for. The person receiving the card would most likely be very excited about such an act of generosity, and would surely make every effort to praise their benefactor and express their gratitude. They would surely value the card and keep it in a safe place.

Probably they would start out by charging something small in order to be assured that the process was really going to work out as stated. But eventually they would start using it whenever they had a need or want. They would be blessed because their needs were met and their benefactor would have the joy that comes with being able to provide those needs.

However, if the person tucked the card away in their wallet and never actually took it out and used it then they would never experience the benefits that their benefactor had intended. They would continue to live as they had before and the benefactor,

---

[1] 2 Peter 1:3
[2] 2 Peter 1:1
[3] John 1:12–13

having provided what was needed, would not receive the joy of seeing their provision accomplish it's intended goal.

Peter says that God has provided everything which pertains to life and godliness. Certainly that pertains to life with Jesus after death. But since the statement says everything it must also apply to life in this world between now and the time the believer dies. The Holy Spirit inspired Paul to write to the Corinthians:

1. that anyone who is in Christ Jesus is a new creature,
2. that the old things have gone away, and
3. that new things have come to them.[1]

Part of the old things and new things pertain to the person's final destination. However, that new creature begins as soon as a person is in Christ.

One of the new things is that the believer has inherited enemies, especially if they go on to becoming a follower of the Way. But they have also been provided with all the tools which God has supplied in order for them to overcome the influence of those enemies and live the life of a new creature which He desires for them. Just as the person who received the credit card needed to *use* the card in order to experience the full benefit of having it, the believer also has to *use* the tools which God has provided in order to experience the new godly life which those tools were designed to provide them with.

---

[1] 2 Corinthians 5:17

image by David Ray Carroll

The Full Armor of God

Ephesians 6:10–13

Finally, be strong in the Lord and in the strength of His might.

Put on the full armor of God, so that you will be able to stand firm against the schemes of the devil.

> For our struggle is not against flesh and blood, but against the rulers, against the powers, against the world forces of this darkness, against the spiritual forces of wickedness in the heavenly places.
>
> Therefore, take up the full armor of God, so that you will be able to resist in the evil day, and having done everything, to stand firm.

First, a follower of the Way will have to learn to lean. The passage does not tell them to be strong in their own strength, but to "be strong in the Lord and in the strength of His might." The follower needs to become strong in a *true* knowledge of their Lord Jesus Christ and learn to lean upon His provisions for the strength to live a godly life.

Then they need to continually remind their self that this passage is not talking about physical armour. The "armor of God" is not physical armor that I can buy at a store and put on over my clothes. The Scriptures reveal an illustration of that concept in the Old Testament story of David and Goliath.[1] Saul offered David the physical armour of this world but David went forth in the name of his God.[2] David realized he was not fighting his own battle, but that the battle belonged to the Lord.[3]

Just as David had to be willing to lean on God's provisions and go[4], so also Paul wrote that it is the responsibility of the believer to "take up the full armor of God," and "to resist in the evil day; and having done everything, to stand firm."

Those three concepts are very important to living the godly life of a new creature:

1. "take up the full armor of God";
2. "resist" the world, the flesh, and the devil; and

---

[1] 1 Samuel 17
[2] verse 45
[3] verses 37, 47
[4] verse 32

3. "stand firm" in following the *Way*, knowing the *truth*, and living the *life*[1] of good works which God has prepared for those who come to Him.[2]

Truth (Reality)

> Ephesians 6:14a
>
> Stand firm therefore, HAVING GIRDED YOUR LOINS [hips] with truth [reality]

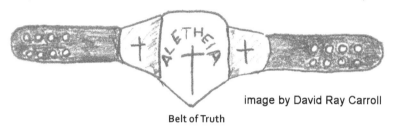

image by David Ray Carroll

Belt of Truth

The Greek word translated here as "truth" is ALETHEIA. To the ancient Greek writers, this word didn't just mean truth as in "to tell the truth." A person can believe something is true and be "telling the truth" when asked about it. This word referred more to the fundamental fact or reality which truth is based upon. It is the opposite of what is ultimately false, fictitious, or an illusion.

The loins refer to the hip area of the body. Whatever physical activity a person does, that is the area of their body that gives them the flexibility to pivot, turn, bend over, etc. When Jacob was wrestling with the angel at Bethel the battle was over when the angel dislocated Jacob's thigh. From that day forward, Jacob walked with a limp.[3]

It is of the utmost importance that every direction in which a follower of the Way turns and whatever activity they are involved in, they remain girded with (or wrapped up in) the truths of God's Word. "The end *never* justifies the means." Even the great men

---

[1] John 14:6
[2] Ephesians 2:10
[3] Genesis 32:25, 31

of the Scriptures were tempted to twist the truth in order to accomplish God's work.

Abraham lost sight of the reality of God's promised protection[1] and was deceptive twice in order to preserve his own life. He was less than truthful first to Pharoah[2] and again to king Abimelech.[3] In both cases the end result was less than favorable for him. Jesus told His disciples that He was the *true reality* at the same time He told them that He was the *way to God*.

Jesus declared that He *is* the living reality, ALETHEIA, which all truth is based upon.[4] That is why it is so important that, in a believer's faith, they continually supply all of the qualities necessary to gain a *true* knowledge of their Lord Jesus the Messiah.[5]

The Apostle John recorded that shortly after He had declared He was the ALETHEIA, Jesus prayed to God the Father for the Apostles at the Last Supper.[6] He mentioned in His prayer that for the sake of His followers He was sanctifying Himself (or, setting Himself aside as the perfect living example of the application of the truths of God's Word to an individual's life). He also stated that He was sanctifying Himself in order that His followers could be sanctified in that same truth. And He asked His Father in Heaven to also sanctify His followers in ALETHEIA because the Word of God is ALETHEIA.

1. begins with saving faith;
2. followed by a commitment to moral excellence;
3. followed by an *accurate* knowledge of God's Word and what it reveals about Jesus;
4. followed by self-control in applying that knowledge through the fruit of a life empowered by the Holy Spirit;
5. applying perseverance whenever falling short of the goal;

---

[1] Genesis 12:3; 15:1
[2] Genesis 12:10–20
[3] Genesis 20:1–18
[4] John 14:6
[5] 2 Peter 1:1–11
[6] John 17:17–19

6. demonstrating godliness as the character of God the Heavenly Father and His Son, Jesus;
7. showing brotherly affection toward other people; and
8. characterizing 1 Corinthians 13 love toward God and all mankind.

Jesus' commitment to His Father lasted up to and through His death and resurrection. In that same manner a follower of the Way's commitment to a growing relationship with God their adoptive Father and Jesus His Son must persevere until they die and go on to actually be in His presence. They must persevere until then in keeping their spiritual loins girded with the truths of God's word and a growing *true* knowledge of Jesus the Christ [Messiah]. Perseverance is not a matter of never falling; it is a matter of getting up, brushing off any accumulation from the fall, and getting back into the game whenever falling or getting knocked down.

Righteousness

Ephesians 6:14b

and HAVING PUT ON THE BREASTPLATE OF RIGHTEOUSNESS,

The breastplate protects the chest and stomach areas. A person's spine and many of their vital organs are in that part of their body. The proper functioning of those body parts is necessary for leading a normal life. In that same way a proper understanding of righteousness is necessary for a believer to live and mature spiritually.

image by David Ray Carroll
Breastplate of Righteousness

The Greek word for righteousness in this passage is

DIKAIOSUNE and the word means a favorable verdict from a court trial. In relationship to a believer's spiritual life, it means that when their Spiritual Father, the God of the heavens and the earth, assesses that person's life on the scales of justice, he gives them a favorable verdict; not because of what they have done, but because of His grace.

> Titus 3:3–8
>
> For we also once were foolish ourselves,
>> disobedient,
>> deceived,
>> enslaved to various lusts and pleasures,
>> spending our life in malice and envy,
>> hateful,
>> hating one another.
>
> But when the kindness of God our Savior and *His* love for mankind appeared, He saved us, not on the basis of deeds which we have done in righteousness, but according to His mercy, by the washing of regeneration and renewing by the Holy Spirit, whom He poured out upon us richly through Jesus Christ our Savior, so that being justified by His grace we would be made heirs [1]according to *the* hope of eternal life.
>
> This is a trustworthy statement; and concerning these things I want you to speak confidently, so that those who have believed God will be careful to engage in good deeds. These things are good and profitable for men.

Just so the readers of Titus don't misunderstand the situation, Paul added that it is "good and profitable for men" to "engage in good deeds." This is very similar to the addition of Ephesians 2:10 after the statement of Ephesians 2:8–9.

Everyone who is a descendant of Adam has to some extent inherited the character qualities listed in Titus 3:3. According to

---

[1] Or *of eternal life according to hope*

the Scriptures, every descendant of Adam will one day die, and after that stand before God at a trial.[1]

According the Scriptures those who have received Jesus as their Savior will not be judged according to their righteousness but according to their faith in His righteousness.[2] God gives them that DIKAIOSUNE judgment not according to anything they have done, but only "according to His mercy." That is what the Scriptures refer to with the term Salvation.

But that is not the end of the story. Salvation also includes "regeneration and renewing by the Holy Spirit, whom He poured out upon us richly through Jesus Christ our Savior." Salvation does not begin at death, but at the moment that a person receives Jesus as their Savior.

It is through that Holy Spirit that a believer is made a new creature[3] and has the ability available to live the "good and profitable" life which God saved them for.[4] That part of a believer's life is referred to by the Scriptures as Sanctification.

It is crucial that a believer has a good grasp on how the "BREASTPLATE OF RIGHTEOUSNESS" works. Understanding the distinction between the righteousness of Salvation and the righteousness of Sanctification will protect the spiritual lungs, heart, spine, and other vital organs from the believer's enemies.

The Gospel Of Peace

Ephesians 6:15

and having shod YOUR FEET WITH THE PREPARATION OF THE GOSPEL OF PEACE;

It is on a believer's feet that they stand firm, and it is on their feet that they go forth to perform whatever good works that God

---

[1] Hebrews 9:27
[2] John 1:12–13; Ephesians 2:8–9; and Titus 3:4–7
[3] 2 Corinthians 5:17
[4] Ephesians 2:10; Titus 3:8

inspires them to do. So wherever they go and whatever they do, they should be doing it on the basis of the "GOSPEL OF PEACE."

The Greek word translated here as "PEACE" is EIRENES and in the original language it has the connotation of wholeness, when all the individual pieces are brought together so that they work well with each other.

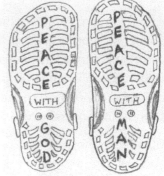

Peace with God

image by David Ray Carroll
Gospel of Peace

> Romans 5:1–2
>
> Therefore, having been justified by faith, [1]we have peace with God through our Lord Jesus Christ, through whom also we have obtained our introduction by faith into this grace in which we stand; and [2]we exult in hope of the glory of God.

> 2 Corinthians 5:17–21
>
> Therefore if anyone is in Christ, [3]*he is* a new creature; the old things passed away; behold, new things have come.
>
> Now all these things are from God, who reconciled us to Himself through Christ and gave us the ministry of reconciliation, namely, that God was in Christ reconciling the world to Himself, not counting their trespasses against them, and [4]He has [5]committed to us the word of reconciliation.

---

[1] Two early mss read *let us have*

[2] Or *let us exult*

[3] Or there is *a new creation*

[4] Lit *having*

[5] Lit *placed in us*

> Therefore, we are ambassadors for Christ, as though God were making an appeal through us; we beg you on behalf of Christ, be reconciled to God. He made Him who knew no sin *to be* sin on our behalf, so that we might become the righteousness of God in Him.

Every believer has been given the wholeness of being at peace with God, not because of anything that they have done, but because of God's grace which they receive through the faith which He supplies.[1] Each believer can now "stand firm" in the peace of that wholeness before God.

Peace within God's family

Every believer is called to walk among their brothers and sisters in the Lord with feet that are wrapped in "THE GOSPEL OF PEACE." One of the seven things the Scriptures declare that God hates is someone who spreads strife between brothers [and/or sisters].[2] Paul gave believers some tips on how to maintain that peace and avoid spreading strife within the family of God their Father.

In his letter to the Corinthians Paul wrote[3] that a believer should:

1. continually rejoice and be glad for God's grace,
2. keep striving for moral excellence,
3. keep comforting each other whenever needed,
4. stay like-minded with Jesus, and
5. live at peace with God and each other.

In his letter to the Thessalonians Paul wrote[4] that a believer should live at peace with other believers by:

1. admonishing those who are slack or disorderly,
2. coming alongside those who are weaker-minded,
3. giving assistance to those who are without adequate strength,

---

[1] Ephesians 2:8–9
[2] Proverbs 6:16–19
[3] 2 Corinthians 13:11
[4] 1 Thessalonians 5:13–16

4. being patient (the first quality of love) toward each other, and
5. always trying to do what is good for everyone even if it is in return for evil.

In both of those letters he writes that all believers should live in EIRENES with one another.

Peace With All Mankind

Paul tells believers that they should not limit walking in peace to their brothers and sisters in the Lord, and gives them some pointers on how that may be accomplished. He wrote to the Roman believers that they should:[1]

1. never do anything evil to anyone who does evil to them,
2. think through what things are considered good in the sight of everyone involved, and
3. (as much as it depends on them) to be at EIRENES with everyone.

Faith

Ephesians 6:16

[2]in addition to all, taking up the shield of faith with which you will be able to extinguish all the flaming arrows of the evil one.

It is faith by which a believer "will be able to extinguish all the flaming arrows of the evil one." Not just by their own faith, but also by the faithfulness of the Son of God who lives in them.[3] The faith that He loves them, and that He has given of Himself (His Holy Spirit) for them.

image by David Ray Carroll

Shield of Faith

---

[1] Romans 12:17–18
[2] Lit *in all*
[3] Galatians 2:20

Satan's temptation of Eve in the garden was that God was not truthful with them and that He was not providing everything that they needed. If she would have used "the shield of faith" and trusted in God's word, as Jesus did in the wilderness, then things would have turned out much different.

If a believer lives their life with faith in what God's word says and trusts in the faithfulness of the Son of God and His love for them[1] then they will be able to recognize and extinguish any flaming arrows of temptation, doubt, lies, or half truths which "the evil one" hurdles their way.

Salvation

Ephesians 6:17a

And take THE HELMET OF SALVATION

Keeping in mind that Salvation is more than just a free escape from punishment is critical to being able to have and keep a clear head. Paul told the Roman followers of the Way to be transformed by the renewing of their minds.[2] Realizing that Salvation and Sanctification are meant by God to go hand-in-hand is part of that transformation. Putting on the pieces of armor and knowing how to use them in order to live the victorious life which God prepared beforehand for Jesus' followers is the other half of the transformation of a believer's mind.

image by David Ray Carroll

Helmet of Salvation

---

[1] Galatians 2:20
[2] Romans 12:2

For Eternity

> Ephesians 2:8–9
>
> For by grace you have been saved through faith; and [1]that not of yourselves, *it is* the gift of God; not as a result of works, so that no one may boast.

For the Here and Now

> Ephesians 2:10
>
> For we are His workmanship,
>> created in Christ Jesus for good works,
>> which God prepared beforehand
>> so that we would walk in them.

> 2 Peter 1:3
>
> His divine power has granted to us everything pertaining to life and godliness,
>
> through the true knowledge of Him who called us [2]by His own glory and [moral] [3]excellence.

The Word Of God

> Ephesians 6:17b
>
> and the sword of the Spirit, which is the word of God.

This is a very important piece of armor. A proper understanding of "the word of God" is essential to knowing how the other pieces of armor operate.

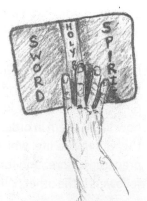

image by David Ray Carroll
Sword of the Spirit

---

[1] I.e. that salvation
[2] Or *to*
[3] Or *virtue*

2 Timothy 3:16–17

All Scripture is [1]inspired by God and
profitable [useful]
 for teaching [doctrines, or what is to be believed],
 for reproof [the test by which something is
 proven true or false, good or bad],
 for correction [restoring to a
 morally excellent state],
 for [2]training [instruction and chastening]
 in righteousness;
so that the man of God may be adequate,
equipped for every good work.

The Scriptures play a very important role in the growth of a believer's relationship with God through His Son Jesus. There are several methods involved in gaining a working knowledge of the Scriptures. They are:

1. Hearing

Ephesians 4:11–16

And He [Jesus] gave
 some *as* apostles,
 and some *as* prophets,
 and some *as* evangelists,
 and some *as* pastors
 and teachers,
for the equipping of the [3]saints
for the work of service,
to the building up of the body of Christ;
 until we all attain to the unity of the faith,
 and of the [4]knowledge of the Son of God,
 to a mature man,

---

[1] Lit *God-breathed*
[2] Lit *training which is in*
[3] Or *holy ones*
[4] Or *true knowledge*

to the measure of the stature [1]which belongs to the fullness of Christ.

[2]As a result, we are no longer to be children,
 tossed here and there by waves
 and carried about by every wind of doctrine,
 by the trickery of men,
 by craftiness [3]in deceitful scheming;
but [4]speaking the truth in love,
 [5]we are to grow up in all *aspects* into Him
 who is the head, *even* Christ,
from whom the whole body,
 being fitted and held together [6]by what every joint supplies,
 according to the [7]proper working of each individual part,
 causes the growth of the body for the building up of itself in love.

Jesus has called out individuals from among His disciples to whom He has given the responsibility of equipping and building up His followers. Preaching, teaching, and discipleship are three ways they perform that responsibility.

One way for a believer to supply knowledge to the determination to be morally excellent[8] is by listening to the pastors, teachers, and mentors whom God brings them into contact with. Then it is the believer's responsibility to do as the Bereans and check out everything that was said against the message of

---

[1] Lit *of the fullness*
[2] Lit *So that we will no longer be*
[3] Lit *with regard to the scheming of deceit*
[4] Or *holding to* or *being truthful in*
[5] Or *let us grow up*
[6] Lit *through every joint of the supply*
[7] Lit *working in measure*
[8] 2 Peter 1:5

the Scriptures to assure that the things they said are so before accepting them as fact.[1]

However, research has verified that even when a person pays attention, they only retain a small percentage of what they hear.

2. Reading

Having a bible available and reading along as a speaker or teacher declares the word also multiplies the retention of the message. Many pastors and teachers now use technology to display the Scriptures they are using so that the people can also read along with them. A bible application on the cell phone is a great asset when a bible is not handy.

Reading along with the speaker helps keep a person's mind on the message and helps them retain more of what has been presented. Several times as much of what is read is retained over what is only listened to. That is because retention increases when more senses (the ears *and* the eyes) are involved.

Jesus repeatedly asked God's people about what they had read in the Scriptures.[2] Paul also commanded that his letters be read in the churches.[3] Paul told his disciple, Timothy, to continually read the Scriptures of the Old Testament to the people.[4] John, the writer of the book of Revelation, declared that there is a special blessing for the person who reads the words of that book and for those who hear the words of that book if they take heed to the things which are written in it.[5]

Moses commanded that each king of Israel should write out for himself a copy of the books that he was writing (the first 5 books of the Bible; Genesis, Exodus, Leviticus, Numbers, and

---

[1] Acts 17:10–11
[2] Matthew 12:3, 5; 19:4; 21:16, 42; 22:31; 24:15; Mark 2:25; 12:10, 26; Luke 6:3; 10:26, etc.
[3] Colossians 4:16; 1 Thessalonians 5:27
[4] 1 Timothy 4:13
[5] Revelation 1:3

Deuteronomy). The king was directed to keep his copies with him and read from them every day for the rest of his life, with the goal of learning from them the fear [or proper respect and reverence] of the Lord his God.[1] It is noteworthy that the king was not just commanded to read through his copies once. He was to continually read from them for the rest of his life.

The Holy Spirit doesn't just zap a believer with all insight and knowledge through one reading of the Scriptures. Every time that they re-read the books of the Bible He reveals more of the meaning and application. No person in this world will ever reach the place where they cannot learn to respect and reverence the Lord their God better by reading through His Scriptures, the Bible, one more time.

Having a reading plan for reading through the Bible on a regular basis is also very helpful. Some of the paraphrases are very helpful in obtaining an overview of the Scriptures written in more of a contemporary style. Many items are available in the marketplace to help the student of the bible gain a deeper knowledge and understanding.

Care must be taken, though, not to use these looser renditions for studying or memorization. For study and memorization it is best to stay with a version that follows as close as possible to the original language.

---

[1] Deuteronomy 17:18–19

3. Studying

The Berean Table

Luke, the writer of the book of Acts, recorded that when Paul and Silas brought the gospel to Berea those who heard were of a much better mind-set because they took the time and made the effort to find out whether what they were hearing was true.[1] They eagerly studied the Scriptures to discern from them what was true. That took effort, and even with all of the study helps a disciple of Jesus has available today it takes a great amount of effort and consistency to properly study the word of God.

A believer in many parts of the world today doesn't have to write their own copy of the Scriptures as Moses commanded. They are readily available to buy. There is, however, much value in writing a copy. It forces the person to pay close attention to each word as they steadily work through the text. Diagraming the book also helps in understanding how the bits of information presented all fit together. That is a very important process for determining the context of the pieces of information. When studying the Scriptures, context is a very important issue, because "a text without a context is a pretext."

---

[1] Acts 17:11

The careful disciple will always be aware of the context and be careful to maintain a proper mind-set in their approach to the Scriptures.

As the disciple listens to what others have to say about the Scriptures, reads the Scriptures, and studies the Scriptures, they should always try to maintain a noble-minded approach to what they accept as truth and what they accept as speculation. A good order for considering context is:

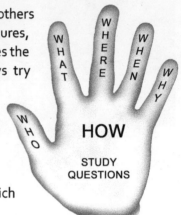

- the sentence(s) in which the text is located;
- the paragraph which contains the sentence;
- the thought the author of the book of the Bible is presenting (this sometimes requires outlining the book);
- the overall message of the book of the Bible, such as

    o who wrote the book,
    o who the author wrote the book to,
    o why they wrote the book (if they stated it – ex., Luke 1:1–4),
    o when the author wrote the book, and
    o any other pertinent information about the book or author; and

- how the book fits into the general message of the Scriptures.

Understanding the context of any Scriptural text is a valuable asset in maintaining that proper mindset and avoiding being led one way then another by every new message or book that comes around declaring something is true.[1]

Studying more than doubles the retention over just hearing and reading.

4. Memorizing

At first a person encouraged to memorize Scripture passages might think it was something that they could never do. There are individuals for which that is true, but take notice of the many other things that the average person memorizes:

- their name, address, and telephone number;
- their military ID number;
- the makes and models of cars;
- the clothes celebrities wear;
- the statistics of different sports figures;
- and even the fishing lure that works best in a particular situation.

Memorizing Scripture passages is very beneficial to a believer's spiritual growth and maturity, just as memorizing the food pyramid is beneficial to physical health.

The prophet Jeremiah, when he was seeking knowledge and understanding about God, wrote that he searched for and devoured His words and they became joyful and delightful to his heart (or inner being) because he wanted to be recognized as being associated with Him.[2] To be a true follower of the Way, a believer must have a true knowledge of Him, and memorizing His words is one step in accomplishing that goal.

The secret to memorization is to begin with the first few words and after they can be said without looking to add a few more until the whole passage can be said. Then it is necessary to review the passage regularly until it can be said naturally.

---

[1] Ephesians 4:14
[2] Jeremiah 15:16

All of what is memorized can be retained when done in conjunction with regular review.

5. Meditating

For the follower of the Way, meditation is not a mystical or religious practice, but simply to ponder God's word as it relates to the circumstances of life. Meditating is thinking carefully about what God has revealed in regard to His wishes and desires, especially before making a decision or reaching a conclusion.

In the Psalms King David revealed the following about meditation:

- the person who delights in God's words and meditates on them around the clock is declared to be a blessed man[1];
- a good time for meditating on God's words is during the night prior to going to sleep or upon awakening[2];
- meditation is also for realizing how God is working and doing things in people's lives and in the world around us[3];

Meditation should not be limited to the Scriptures, but to everything relating to God. It is not just what a believer chooses to think about at specific times, but it is making God part of all of their thinking.

Joshua was to take over from Moses and lead God's people into the Promised Land. But God told him that his first priority was to meditate on how God's words related to himself personally. Then he would be prosperous and have good success in the mission which God was calling him to do.[4] That same principle holds true today for followers of the Way.

---

[1] Psalm 1:2; 119:48
[2] Psalm 4:4; 63:6
[3] Psalm 77:12; 143:5; 145:5
[4] Joshua 1:8

That is not the natural method because it is much easier for a believer to see the need for teaching, reproof, correction, and training in righteousness[1] in other people than to see them in their own life. Jesus referred to that principle in the Sermon on the Mount when He told those who were following Him that they should first focus on correcting the things in their own life so that they could better see how to help others.[2]

Meditation is shown in the thumb because the thumb is used in conjunction with the operation of each of the fingers. In that same way meditation is listed last in this list, but is properly used in conjunction with hearing, reading, studying, and memorizing in the life of a follower of the Way.

Handling the Word of God

If a believer is to be prosperous and have good success in God's work, then they must apply their meditations first and foremost to their own life, and then to those whom God has given them an influence upon.

> Hebrews 4:12–16
>
> For the word of God is
> > living
> > and active
> > and sharper than any two-edged sword,
> > > and piercing as far as the division
> > > of soul and spirit,
> > > of both joints and marrow,
> > and able to judge

---

[1] 2 Timothy 3:16
[2] Matthew 7:3–5

the thoughts
and intentions of the heart.

And there is no creature hidden from His sight, but all things are open and laid bare to the eyes of Him with whom we have to do.

Therefore, since we have a great high priest who has passed through the heavens, Jesus the Son of God, let us hold fast our confession. For we do not have a high priest who cannot sympathize with our weaknesses, but One who has been tempted in all things as *we are, yet* without sin.

Therefore let us draw near with confidence to the throne of grace, so that we may receive mercy and find grace to help in time of need.

Chapter 9

Prayers Of A Follower Of The Way

> Ephesians 6:18–20
>
> [1]With all prayer and petition [2]pray at all times in the Spirit,
>
> and with this in view, [3]be on the alert with all perseverance and petition for all the saints,
>
> and *pray* on my behalf, that utterance may be given to me in the opening of my mouth, to make known with boldness the mystery of the gospel, for which I am an ambassador in [4]chains; that [5]in *proclaiming* it I may speak boldly, as I ought to speak.

Simply stated, prayer is communication, spirit to Spirit, with God the Father and Jesus the Lord, realizing their presence as the believer walks in the way of this life. This first phrase, "With all prayer [PROSEUCHE, exchanging of thoughts and ideas] and petition [DEESIS, asking for felt needs] pray [PROSEUCHOMAI, exchange thoughts and ideas] at all times in the Spirit" literally means, "With all exchanging of thoughts and ideas and asking for felt needs, communicate with God continually in the Spirit."

A believer directs their spiritual communication toward God in Heaven and He communicates to them through His Spirit which dwells in their inner being, impressing the thoughts of their mind as they direct the intent of their heart to know and hear His words. Jesus told His disciples that He would request His Father to send the Holy Spirit to be in the inner being of His followers forever.[6] That

---

[1] Lit *Through*
[2] Lit *praying*
[3] Lit *being*
[4] Lit *a chain*
[5] Two early mss read *I may speak it boldly*
[6] John 14:16–17

is how they are directed by the first part of this passage to conduct their personal prayer life; continually realizing God's presence and communicating with Him about everything that is happening.

That communication takes place between their spirit and the Spirit of God, and is supposed to be a continual around-the-clock "at all times" awareness of His presence and their ability to communicate with Him. Paul wrote in his first letter to the believers in Thessalonica that they were to pray continually, without ceasing.[1] The two Greek words which are translated "pray continually, without ceasing" in the passage are ADIALEIPTOS PROSEUCHESTHAY which literally mean "unceasingly stay in communication with God."

Paul then expanded the focus of a believer's prayers to include "all the saints." The phrase which Paul uses, "be on the alert", is the Greek word AGRUPNEO, which literally means "not being asleep." Not daydreaming, but being aware of what is going on around them. The Greek word used here for "perseverance" is not the same word used in 2 Peter 1:6. This time the word is PROSKARTERESIS, which means "to constantly make whatever effort is needed in order to prevail."

And on behalf of those who are actively carrying forth the gospel, Paul requests that believers pray for the proper words to be given to them whenever they open their mouth so that they may boldly profess the mysteries of the gospel message. The word used for "boldness" is PARRESIA, which actually means "to speak in clearness and earnestness" with the connotation that what is spoken should be taken seriously.

When Paul wrote his first letter to Timothy, he included two other forms of prayer.

> 1 Timothy 2:1–2
>
> First of all, then, I urge that
>   entreaties [DEESIS, asking for felt needs] *and*

---

[1] 1 Thessalonians 5:17

> prayers [PROSEUCHE, exchanging of thoughts and ideas],
> petitions [ENTEUXIS, intercession
> (2 Corinthians 5:20)] *and*
> thanksgivings [EUCHARISTIA, expressions of thankfulness],
> be made on behalf of all men, for kings and all who are in [1]authority, so that we may lead a tranquil and quiet life in all godliness and [2]dignity.

Therefore, Paul says that a believer should:

- maintain a continual state of spiritual communication with their Father in heaven;
- not be daydreaming but stay alert to what is happening in the lives of other people and constantly make whatever effort is needed in order to prevail in helping them and communicating with their Father in Heaven about needs they feel those people have;
- intercede on other people's behalf in order that they would make whatever changes are needed for them to be reconciled to God (2 Corinthians 5:20 – following God's direction to help others hit the mark of godliness), either by salvation or sanctification;
- pray for those who are actively involved in carrying forth the gospel that the words would be given to them by the Holy Spirit so that they would impress the hearers to realize the gospel should be taken seriously; and
- be diligent in expressing their heartfelt thanksgiving to God and Jesus for everything that They do.

A section on prayer is not complete without the basics for a believer's communications with their Father in heaven which Jesus gave in the Sermon on the Mount:

---

[1] Or *a high position*
[2] Or *seriousness*

Basic 1 – Prayer Is Personal Communication

Matthew 6:5–6 –
[Jesus speaking at the Sermon on the Mount]

"When you pray,
> you are not to be like the hypocrites;
>> for they love to stand and pray
>> in the synagogues and on the street corners
>> [1]so that they may be seen by men.
> Truly I say to you, they have their reward in full.

But you, when you pray,
> go into your inner room,
> close your door and
> pray to your Father who is in secret,
and your Father who sees *what is done* in secret will reward you."

The Greek word which is translated "hypocrites" here is the antonym for the word translated "sincere" in 1 Timothy 1:5, "But the goal of our instruction is love from a pure heart and a good conscience and a sincere faith." The word was commonly used by the Greeks in reference to an actor on a stage, or behind a mask; someone who is playing a part.

Paul wrote to his disciple Timothy that the goal for a follower of the Way is 1 Corinthians 13 type "love [which flows] from a pure heart and a good conscience and a [un-hypocritical] faith." A follower of the Way's goal is to have a faith that is transparent (the same on the inside as on the outside).

In context, Jesus had just finished defining the law as pertaining to the thoughts and intents of the heart, not just the actions of an individual. Then He warned against doing good deeds in order to impress other people and gain their honor; but instead to do them secretly before their Father who sees and rewards His children.

---

[1] Lit *to be apparent to men*

Jesus then placed the prayer life of His followers in that same category.

According to Jesus, a believer's prayer life is something that is to be a communication between their Father in heaven and His child on earth; nothing more, and nothing less. That privacy may be a literal private place or the privacy of their inner being, directing their thoughts to their Father who searches their heart and understands the intents behind their thoughts (1 Chronicles 28:9).

That is not a limitation of the physical place for all their prayers to the privacy of an inner room; but rather a direction about the purpose and focus of those prayers; as in the rest of the context. The *focus* of a believer's prayers is to be their "Father who is in secret", not "in the synagogues and on the street corners"; and the *purpose* is to be so their "Father who sees what is done in secret will reward [them]" by letting them find Him in a growing personal relationship, not "so that [they] may be seen by men."

Whenever Jesus or His followers did pray before men their prayers were always a personal communication with their Father in heaven and the purpose for being public was not to "be seen by men" but for the edification of the hearers.

Basic 2 – Prayer Is For Relationship Building

Matthew 6:7–8 –
[Jesus speaking at the Sermon on the Mount]

"And when you are praying,
    do not use meaningless repetition
    as the Gentiles do,
    for they suppose that they will be heard
    for their many words.
So do not be like them;
for your Father knows what you need
before you ask Him."

God already knows all about each of His believers. When they pray, they are not telling Him anything that He does not already know. So their prayers are not about giving God knowledge about anything. Their prayers are important to God because they are their communication with Him. Communication is a major part of building any relationship because it is communication which brings all of the other parts of the relationship together. If a believer is going to grow in their adopted child / Father in heaven relationship with God through His natural son Jesus Christ then there must be an atmosphere of honest and meaningful communication between them.

Throughout this basic teaching on prayer, Jesus uses the term Father whenever He refers to God. It is as though He wants His followers to realize that a Father / child relationship is what the God of heaven and earth wishes to develop with each one of them and their individual prayer life is supposed to be the communications within that relationship.

There is an example of the difference between relational prayer and performance prayer in the encounter between Elijah and the priests of Baal.[1] As a prophet of the living God, Elijah already had an active private and public prayer life with the Lord. Because of that relationship he was able to confidently challenge the priests to call on their gods and he would call on YAHWEH; and the one who answers would be the true God.[2]

- The priests of Baal prayed all morning, leaping all around their altar, and at noon Baal had not answered them one peep.[3]
- At noon, Elijah taunted them by telling them that they should speak louder, because Baal is not of this world and may be busy. He might be occupied with something else,

---

[1] 1 Kings 18
[2] 1 Kings 18:24
[3] 1 Kings 18:26

or might be gone on a trip somewhere, or might even be asleep and they need to awaken him.[1]
- So the priests of Baal shouted as loud as they could all afternoon They even cut themselves with knives and spears so that they bled, which was likely part of their manner of worshiping Baal. However, come evening their god had not even paid any attention to all their commotion.[2]
- Then Elijah simply arose and spoke so that the people could hear him (a public prayer). He personally asked YAHWEH to glorify Himself and declare that He is the God of His people, and to turn their hearts back to Himself.[3]

Another good example of a public prayer is given by Jesus when He prayed before His disciples at the Last Supper.[4] In both instances the prayers were made in public, not to bring glory upon the person giving the prayer, but to glorify the God to whom they were praying and to bring edification to the people whom they were praying before.

Basic 3 – A Model Prayer

Matthew 6:9–15 –
[Jesus speaking at the Sermon on the Mount]

"Pray, then, in this way:
'Our Father who is in heaven,
Hallowed be Your name.
Your kingdom come.
Your will be done,
On earth as it is in heaven.
Give us this day [5]our daily bread.
And forgive us our debts,
as we also have forgiven our debtors.

---

[1] 1 Kings 18:27
[2] 1 Kings 18:28–29
[3] 1 Kings 18:36–37
[4] John 17
[5] Or *our bread for tomorrow*

> And do not lead us into temptation,
> But deliver us from [1]evil.
> [2][For Yours is the kingdom and the power and the glory forever. Amen.]'
>
> For if you forgive [3]others for their transgressions, your heavenly Father will also forgive you.
>
> But if you do not forgive [4]others, then your Father will not forgive your trespasses."

Jesus had just told His followers not to "use meaningless repetition" in their communication to God, so He did not give this prayer for them to just repeat to their Father. Instead, He gave it to them as a model for the way in which they should approach their Heavenly Father in conversation. Each section reveals something about the way He wanted His followers to converse with their God:

- [Their] Father who is in heaven [Approach God on an adopted child / Father basis],
- Hallowed be Your name [Set His name, YAHWEH, apart in the believer's life above all others as holy].
- Your kingdom come [Eagerly await the coming of His Son Jesus to rule His kingdom]
- Your will be done [The Father's will always takes precedence over the child's],
- On earth as it is in heaven [Be committed to Moral Excellence in this life on earth].
- Give [them] this day [their] daily bread [If they have food and covering today, with these they will be content[5]].
- And forgive [them their] debts [Realize how much they owe Jesus for the grace He has shown them],

---

[1] Or *the evil one*
[2] This clause not found in early mss
[3] Gr *anthropoi*
[4] Gr *anthropoi*
[5] 1 Timothy 6:8

- as [they] also have forgiven [their] debtors [Realize that they need to show grace to those who become indebted to them].
- And do not lead [them] into temptation [Know that no temptation comes from their Father in heaven[1]],
- But deliver [them] from evil [Whenever they are tempted they will look for the way God has provided for them to escape;[2] and they will be careful not to willingly submit themselves to temptation].
- For Yours is the kingdom and the power and the glory forever [Be faithful to live as a citizen in their Father's kingdom; rely upon His Spirit for power and leading; and be careful to always give Him the glory for their life].

The word "transgressions" is a translation of the Greek word PARAPTOMA which literally means "to be close and then move away." It is typically translated as "sins", "transgressions", "trespasses", "offenses", or the likes since each can represent a departure from a close relationship with God and doing what promotes the growth of that relationship. The word "debts" in the prayer is a translation of the Greek word OPHEILEMA and means "the repayment of indebtedness." In each case the word translated "forgive" is the Greek word APHIEMI which literally means "to put or send away."

So what Jesus is saying in those two sentences is that the believer's Father in heaven will treat their relationship with Him in the same way that they treat their relationships with other people. That is a very important concept if prayer is considered to be an integral part of a growing Father / child relationship with God.

The truths contained in these passages are the foundation for a life of prayer. They provide the framework for a life of constant communication between a follower of the Way and God.

---

[1] James 1:13
[2] 1 Corinthians 10:13

Epilogue

WARNING!!! This book is not meant to replace reading and studying the Bible. I have gone to great lengths to keep the scripture passages which I referenced within their proper context, but their best context is the book in which they are written. And that book's best context is the collection of books which are contained in the Bible. My purpose for this book is to introduce my readers to the One who inspired the writers of those books, and to give them a foundation for understanding the common theme which permeates those writings.

Two of my foster fathers were masons in the building trades. I learned from them that the first part of laying up a wall is to mortar the corner stones (usually bricks, cement blocks, etc.) in place. The placement of those corner stones must be as accurate as possible because a line stretched between them is used to align all of the wall stones. If the wall is to be located properly the corner stones must first be aligned properly. If the wall is to end up the right height and level then the corner stones must be the right height and level with each other.

The writer of Acts describes a time when Peter was talking to the rulers and elders of Israel in Jerusalem. Filled with the Holy Spirit, he described Jesus as the main corner stone of their religion.[1] That is the corner stone on which all of the other stones of the wall will be aligned if the other parts of the building are to be properly fitted together.

The Apostle Paul, in his letter to the Ephesians, described followers of the Way as a Spiritual dwelling of God, built on the foundation of the apostles and prophets with Jesus the Messiah as the corner stone.[2] Both Peter and Paul viewed Jesus as the corner stone from which the building of our faith is built.

---

[1] Acts 4:8–11
[2] Ephesians 2:19–22

The proper foundation for what God is doing today is the messages which He delivered through inspiration of the apostles and prophets. We are part of God's household (His children). In other words, we are the walls of the building.

To be properly fitted together, we must be properly aligned with Jesus. To be properly aligned with Jesus we must have a *true* knowledge of who He is and what He taught. I believe that is why God inspired the Apostle Peter to write his second letter to the followers of the way who had been dispersed back to their home lands after the persecution which began with the stoning of Stephen.

I believe that God inspired me to write this book, but the words of this book are not inspired in the same sense as the books of the Bible are inspired. Knowing that I am in the latter part of my life here, I have simply attempted to share with you, the reader, what God has taught me in the last 60 years since I began to align myself with Jesus and become a member of God's family.

Imagine with me that this book is the lobby of an office building and there are seven doors leading from the lobby into individual rooms. You have been in the lobby while you read the pages of this book, but now it is time to make a decision.

Where are you in life according to having a true knowledge of Jesus, the main corner stone?

What are your needs for obtaining a more true knowledge of Jesus, the main corner stone?

In this book you were presented with the way to be a follower of the Way. There is a receptionist in the lobby. The receptionist's question is simply, "Are you a follower of the Way?" If not, then you are encouraged to have a seat here in the lobby and re-read the sections about becoming a follower of Jesus, the Way. If you are already a follower of Jesus then the receptionist encourages you to consider your life, and choose the door that represents your greatest need right now:

116

image by David Ray Carroll

The Lobby at the Building of Our Faith

- Door #1 – Make a commitment to Moral Excellence. Not just acting morally but being a moral person.
- Door #2 – Know the truth. Know the difference between the facts of God's word and the speculations of men. In the first book of the Bible, Satan came to Adam and Eve with the truth of God's word but then added his speculations as though they were also true. The last book of the Bible declares that the blessings of the book go to those who hear, read, and obey the things which are written in it.[1] Know, and keep your concentration on, the words of the Bible in their context, not just the theologies and speculations which men have created from them.
- Door #3 – Begin applying Self Control to obey the things which are written in the Bible and apply them to your life. A good place to start is by removing anything you may be doing or thinking that is found in Appendix A from your life and adding the virtues listed in Appendix C. Remember that Jesus sent His Spirit to dwell within you to empower you for this task. But you need to appropriate that power. Jesus sent His Spirit to dwell in His followers and give them the wisdom and power to live a victorious life. Paul said

---

[1] Revelation 1:3

117

that if you are walking in the power of the Spirit of God then you will not be doing the desires of the flesh.[1] The principle behind this door is simple: live by the lusts of the flesh and the deeds of the flesh will control you; walk by the Spirit of God and the fruits of the Spirit will control you. Each person who is a believer has those two dogs (the lusts of the flesh and the Spirit of God) inside them while they are in this life. The dog that wins the fight is the one you feed.

- Door #4 – Exhibit Perseverance. You will have failures. That is why a commitment to Moral Excellence is the first door. That door may have to be entered numerous times, but you must also realize that you cannot win the battle with only a commitment. Perseverance, or keeping on keeping on, is a necessary element to finishing the race.
- Door #5 – Godliness. Allow the fruits of the Spirit listed in Appendix B to show through in your life.
- Door #6 – Brotherly Affection. Remember that you are a brother to every human being. On top of that, you are a brother in arms to every other follower of the Way. Put on the full armor of God, and help your brothers any way you can to put on and use their armor.
- Door #7 – Love. Everything you do, do it according to Appendix C.

Review the descriptions of these doors in the book. You may enter and exit any of these doors as often as you wish. Leave the door open when you exit and make what you learned there a regular part of who you are. The promise is that if the contents of these doors are increasingly becoming a part of what you are really like then you will be continually gaining in a true knowledge of your Lord and be constantly more useful to Him for His work in this world.[2]

---

[1] Galatians 5:16
[2] 2 Peter 1:8

1 Peter 3:8–17

[1]To sum up, all of you [followers of the Way] be
    harmonious,
    sympathetic,
    brotherly,
    kindhearted, and
    humble in spirit;
    not returning evil for evil or insult for insult,
    but [2]giving a blessing instead;
for you were called for the very purpose that you might
inherit a blessing.

For,
    "THE ONE WHO DESIRES LIFE,
    TO LOVE AND SEE GOOD DAYS,
    MUST KEEP HIS TONGUE FROM EVIL
    AND HIS LIPS FROM SPEAKING DECEIT.
    HE MUST TURN AWAY FROM EVIL AND DO GOOD;
    HE MUST SEEK PEACE AND PURSUE IT.
    FOR THE EYES OF THE LORD
    ARE TOWARD THE RIGHTEOUS,
    AND HIS EARS ATTEND TO THEIR PRAYER,
    BUT THE FACE OF THE LORD
    IS AGAINST THOSE WHO DO EVIL."

Who is [3]there to harm you if you prove zealous for what
is good? But even if you should suffer for the sake of
righteousness, you [4]are blessed.

AND DO NOT FEAR THEIR [5]INTIMIDATION,
AND DO NOT BE TROUBLED, but
    [6]sanctify Christ as Lord in your hearts,

---

[1] Or *Finally*

[2] Lit *blessing instead*

[3] Lit *the one who will harm you*

[4] Or *would be*

[5] Lit *fear*

[6] I.e. set apart

always *being* ready to make a [1]defense to everyone
who asks you to give an account for the hope that
is in you,
yet with gentleness and [2]reverence;
[3]and keep a good conscience so that in the thing in
which you are slandered, those who revile your good
behavior in Christ will be put to shame.
For it is better, if [4]God should will it so, that you suffer
for doing what is right rather than for doing what is
wrong.

I cannot write an ending for this book any better than Peter scribed
in this passage, so with that admonition I will call it, "The End."

---

[1] Or *argument;* or *explanation*

[2] Or *fear*

[3] Lit *having a good*

[4] Lit *the will of God*

Meet The Author

Richard Ray Beavo

I first heard about God and the stories of the Scriptures through the children's ministry of a small village church. At the age of fourteen I received Jesus and became an adopted son of God when my eighth grade teacher explained the good news of the Gospel to me. Years later I was approached by my pastor and invited to take part in a one-on-one discipleship ministry. There I began to grow in my personal relationship with God my Father through Jesus His Son. Just an everyday follower of Jesus, I searched for and found the reality of a dynamic personal relationship with the God of the Bible. I have served my Lord in many capacities including Sunday School Teacher, Sunday School Superintendent, Word of Life Olympians leader, Missions Committee Chairperson, Christian Education Elder, and Elder Board Chairman. I have also been involved in Prison and Juvenile Facility ministries. Presently involved in one-on-one discipleship and Bible studies, my passion is to share what God has shown me during my sixty plus years as a son of God.

Appendix A

Galatians 5:19–21

Now the deeds of the flesh are evident, which are:

Deed	Greek word
[1]immorality,	πορνεία (por-ni'-ah)
fornication, whoredom, sexual relations between unmarried persons	
impurity,	ἀκαθαρσία (ak-ath-ar-see'-ah)
uncleanness, impurity, in a moral sense: the impurity of lustful, luxurious, profligate living	
sensuality,	ἀσέλγεια (as-elg'-i-a)
wantonness (sexually immodest or promiscuous); carnality, as filthy words, indecent bodily movements, unchaste handling of males and females, etc	
Idolatry,	εἰδωλολατρία (i-do-lol-at-ri'-ah)
service to or worship of an image, idol, or false god	
Sorcery,	φαρμακεία (far-mak-i'-ah)
magic, witchcraft, wizardry, enchantment (being under a spell)	
enmities,	ἔχθραι (ekh'-thrai)
hostility or alienation (isolation from a group or an activity to which one should belong or in which one should be involved)	
strife,	ἔρις (er'-is)
to be quarrelsome, contentious, loving to dispute, wrangling	
jealousy,	ζῆλος (dzay'-los)
an inner bubbling of resentment or envy (like boiling water), used negatively here as jealousy and in some other places positively as zeal	
outbursts of anger,	Θυμοί (thy-moi')

---

[1] I.e. sexual immorality

Deed	Greek word
outbursts of passion or anger, fits of rage	
disputes,	ἐριθεῖαι (er-ith-ei'-ai)
(the seeking of followers and adherents by means of gifts, the seeking of followers, hence) ambitions, rivalrys, self-seeking; causing feuds or factions	
dissensions,	διχοστασίαι (dee-khos-tas-ee'-ai)
properly, standing separately; dividing people into pointless disagreements that lead to discord	
[1]factions,	αἱρέσεις (hah'-ee-res-is)
properly, self-chosen opinions; sects, heresies	
Envying,	φθόνοι (fthon'-oi)
a feeling of ill-will which embitters the soul over time	
drunkenness,	μέθαι (meth'-ai)
intoxication, losing control of one's facilities or behavior	
carousing,	κῶμοι (ko'-moi)
riotous revelry, drinking festivities	

and things like these,

of which I forewarn you, just as I have forewarned you, that those who practice such things will not inherit the kingdom of God.

---

[1] Or *heresies*

Appendix B

Galatians 5:22–23

But the fruit of the Spirit is

Deed	Greek word
love,	ἀγάπη (ag-ah'-pay)
a commitment which centers on moral excellence (2 Peter 1:5) and results in the character and conduct described in 1 Corinthians 13	
joy,	χαρά (khar-ah')
the awareness of God's grace – Ephesians 2:8–10	
peace,	εἰρήνη (i-ray'-nay)
from the root "to join", being joined together with each other and God through Jesus Christ	
patience,	μακροθυμία (mak-roth-oo-mee'-ah)
the inner power of restraint, particularly when faced with suffering, opposition, or retaliation for a wrong suffered which comes from submission to God's will for my life	
kindness,	χρηστότης (khray-stot'-ace)
the kind attitude towards others that is useful and profitable in displaying the Gospel of Christ Jesus to others	
goodness,	ἀγαθωσύνη (ag-ath-o-soo'-nay)
the necessary quality which displays God's goodness, who "causes His sun to rise on the evil and the good, and sends rain on the righteous and the unrighteous." (Matthew 5:45)	
faithfulness,	πίστις (pis'-tis)
the firm persuasion and conviction of things hoped for but not seen, which is a gift of God (Hebrews 11:1,6; Ephesians 2:8)	
gentleness,	πραΰτης (prah-oo'-tace)
being strong yet kind, tender, and mild-mannered; the balance of strength and severity which comes from God's control	

Deed	Greek word
self-control;	ἐγκράτεια (eng-krat'-i-ah)
a mastery, restraint, control, or continence which comes from within but is not self-generated but God-generated	

against such things there is no law.

Appendix C

1 Corinthians 13:4–7

Quality	Greek word
Love is patient,	μακροθυμεῖ (mak-roth-yoo'-mei)
exhibits the inner power of restraint, particularly when faced with suffering, opposition, or retaliation for a wrong suffered	
love is kind and	χρηστεύεται (khraste-yoo'-e-tai)
is kind in a helpful sense, gentle	
is not jealous;	ζηλοῖ (dzay-loi')
doesn't have an inner bubbling of resentment or envy (like boiling water), used negatively here as jealousy and in some other places positively as zeal	
love does not brag and	περπερεύεται (per-per-yoo'-e-tai)
isn't boastful, excessively self-praising	
is not arrogant,	φυσιοῦται (foo-see-ou'-tai)
isn't puffed up, or blown up; from the root "to inflate by blowing into, as a balloon"	
does not act unbecomingly;	ἀσχημονεῖ (as-kay-mon-ei')
doesn't act improperly for one who claims to be a follower of Jesus, and a child of God	
it does not seek its own,	ζητεῖ τὰ ἑαυτῆς (dzay-tei' ta heh-au-tēs')
doesn't seek, desire, or demand its own things (1 Corinthians 10:24)	
is not provoked,	Παροξύνεται (par-ox-oo'-ne-tai)
isn't easily aroused or incited to anger or irritation	
does not take into account a wrong suffered,	λογίζεται κακόν (log-iz'-e-tai kak-on')
doesn't keep an account, or reckon, or consider, the wrong, bad, or evil things done by others	

Quality	Greek word
does not rejoice in unrighteousness,	χαίρει ἐπὶ ἀδικίᾳ (khai'-rei epi ad-ee-kee'-ah)
doesn't rejoice, or be glad, at injustice or unrighteousness	
but rejoices with the truth;	συνχαίρει ἀληθείᾳ (syng-khai'-rei al-ay'-thi-a)
rejoices, or is glad, with a true principle or belief, especially one of fundamental importance	
1bears all things,	πάντα στέγει (panta steg'-ei)
covers up, hides and excuses all of the errors and faults of others	
believes all things,	πάντα πιστεύει (panta pist-teu'-ei)
in an ethical sense, has all confidence in the goodness of others	
hopes all things,	πάντα ἐλπίζει (panta el-pi'-zei)
waits for all things, including salvation, with all confidence	
endures all things.	πάντα ὑπομένει (panta hoop-om-en'-ei)
remains against, bravely and calmly bears up against, or perseveres against all obstacles.	

---

1 Or *covers*

127

Scripture Index

CPSIA information can be obtained
at www.ICGtesting.com
Printed in the USA
BVHW031016060919
557777BV00006B/31/P